Jaguar XJS

Jaguar XJS

A collector's guide
by Paul Skilleter

MOTOR RACING PUBLICATIONS LTD
Unit 6, The Pilton Estate, 46 Pitlake, Croydon CR0 3RY, England

First published 1996

British Library Cataloguing in Publication Data

Skilleter, Paul, 1945–
   Jaguar XJS : a collector's guide
   1. Jaguar XJS automobile 2. Jaguar XJS automobile
Collectors and collecting
I. Title
629.2'222

ISBN 0-947981-99-3

Typeset by Richard Clark, Penzance, Cornwall
Printed in Great Britain by The Amadeus Press Ltd,
Huddersfield, West Yorkshire

Contents

Introduction and acknowledgements

Little did I suspect during the XJ-S's 1975 press launch that over 20 years later I would still be driving and writing about the car as a current model! Yet the XJ-S became Jaguar's most successful sporting model ever, surviving into its 21st year with honour.

Nor will the intentionally more sporting XK8 directly replace it; the XJ-S remains unique in Jaguar's history as a Grand Touring car in the traditional sense, with comfort and size as important as mere efficiency.

These pages give a straightforward account of the XJ-S' production career in perhaps more detail than has been attempted before. I have also tried to convey what it is like to drive and live with the various types. It is also intended as a tribute to the men who conceived the XJ-S: Sir William Lyons and his brilliant 1960s team, including Malcolm Sayer, Bill Heynes and Bob Knight.

This book evolved from part of the *Collector's Guide* on the XJ-Series Jaguars (first published in 1984) and I must thank again those from Jaguar who helped me with that title, notably Doug Thorpe, Paul Walker, Ian Luckett and the late David Boole. Andrew Whyte, undoubtedly the world's greatest Jaguar historian, who alas died in 1988, also helped with pictures and advice.

In preparing this virtually all-new title I am very grateful to David Crisp, of Jaguar's PR department, former chief chassis engineer Tom Jones and, once more, David Boole, Jaguar's PR director until his recent sad and untimely death. Jim Patten, freelance writer and assistant editor of *Jaguar World* magazine, helped with many invaluable photographs.

I must also single out Ray Ingman, of Classic Spares, Waltham Cross, for giving me the benefit of his immense 'hands on' knowledge of the XJ-S; nearly all the practical information covering assessment, maintenance and modification comes from Ray, who also distilled the essential production changes for an Appendix. These changes were researched in great depth by Ron Sotherton, parts manager of the Jaguar dealers Grange Motors, of Brentwood, Essex. I cannot thank these two enthusiastic professionals enough!

Finally, some apologies: to my family, for many long winter evenings and weekends I have spent closeted with the word processor, and to publisher John Blunsden, for a succession of missed deadlines...

The XJ-S enjoyed a long and honourable career, and if its merits become clearer to you after reading this book, I will have achieved my ambition!

February 1996   PAUL SKILLETER

CHAPTER 1

Jaguar creates a Grand Tourer

XJ-S design and development

The XJ-S has aroused more comment and criticism than almost any other car from the Lyons stable – with the possible exception of the original SS 1 of 1931! Its styling was controversial and the whole concept of the car – a 2-plus-2 measuring almost 16ft stem to stern and having a 14mpg thirst – was questionable to many even at the 1975 launch. Yet, despite a shaky start, the XJ-S became Jaguar's most successful sporting model, with a production total far exceeding that of the E-type.

Initially, the XJ-S suffered from preconceptions. Although controlled leaks from Coventry hinted to the contrary, expectations were high that Jaguar would produce a true successor to the E-type – a 'real' sportscar, relatively compact and available in open as well as closed form. Instead, Jaguar chose to follow another branch of their evolutionary tree, and what emerged at the Frankfurt show in September 1975 was radically different: a big, luxury GT with no soft-top option. Worse, its styling did not meet with the usual acclaim. Also, it was a very expensive motor car; for the first time, at £8,900 a Jaguar cost as much as a Ferrari…

Yet given the role which Jaguar had determined for it, the XJ-S was superbly competent, and even those who were critical of its styling were usually won over after a spell at the wheel. With such outstanding performance, refinement and poise there to enjoy, what did a slightly oversize bodyshell and possibly quirky styling matter? As a Grand Tourer the XJ-S had rivals, but no equals; no other car in the world could be driven as fast, as smoothly and as quietly over long distances. A lot could be forgiven in exchange for qualities like those!

The XJ-S story began in the late 1960s when serious thought was given to an E-type replacement. Even then there was no real indication that Jaguar ever contemplated its traditional return to basics when designing its new sporting car – largely because of the new type of customer to be targetted. This time it was not the sportscar enthusiast, but the more affluent 35 to 55-year-old, whose car would probably be provided (in the UK at least) by his company. As Jaguar stated at the time: 'Few firms are likely to see it as being in the company's interests to buy very small passenger capacity, possibly unreliable, sportscars, but they may be persuaded towards a close-coupled, relatively refined motor car with a dignified but aggressive aspect.'

Nevertheless Jaguar completed an in-depth feasibility study of the then increasingly fashionable mid-engined configuration that the company itself had used for the stillborn XJ13 Le Mans car of 1967. But it was rejected for the new GT because of doubts that a mid-engined vehicle could meet frontal crash test standards, and because the theoretical handling and traction benefits did not outweigh practical disadvantages in passenger and luggage 'packaging'. It would also have required unique and expensive componentry. So while the E-type of 1961 had reverted to an XK 120-type strict two-seater format, rather than continuing the 2-plus-2 XK 150 theme, XJ27 (as the new car was coded) very definitely carried on from where the highly successful 2-plus-2 long-wheelbase E-type left off.

This slotted in with the decision to use the recently introduced XJ saloon as a base, cost-effectively sharing its

Jaeger fashion models unveil the XJ-S in London in September 1975; but the shape and size of the new sporting Jaguar came as a shock to those expecting an E-type replacement.

mechanical components and taking advantage of its superb refinement, handling and production-proven reliability. This did determine the new sporting Jaguar's minimum size and weight, though, and the 'sporting' aspects of the new car were further pushed back when, in common with most other manufacturers, Jaguar believed that regulations would soon outlaw all open cars in the United States. As it happened, these proposals were scotched in 1974, but by that time, of course, the XJ-S was on the point of announcement – in coupe form only.

The first prototype XJ27 was built in 1969 on a 102in-wheelbase version of the normal (108in-wheelbase) XJ saloon floorpan; two styling versions were produced, one by Jaguar's mainstream styling department, the other by Malcolm Sayer, with a degree of input from Sir William himself (who continued to advise on styling 'in a consultative capacity' after his retirement in 1972. But there was never much doubt that, as a protege of both Lyons and Heynes, Sayer would win.

His ideas for the new GT car differed radically from those expressed in his previous sportscar designs, the C, D and E-types. Gone were most of the beautifully blended curves, replaced by a mainly flat bonnet, chopped-off rear end and rather less rotund sides. But the most distinctive feature of the new design was, of course, the 'flying buttress' treatment aft of the side windows.

These swept down from the roof and, curving gently inwards, blended into the tail and rear wings, almost enclosing the shallow, near-vertical rear window. Almost certainly they were inspired by the Italian coachbuilding fashions prevailing in the 1960s, and perhaps in particular by the 206GT and 246GT Dino Ferraris, with their Pininfarina-designed bodywork developed from a styling exercise by the same house and exhibited – complete with sports-racing-style flying buttresses – at the Paris show of 1965. Sayer had even incorporated them on a purely experimental mock-up on the 2-plus-2 E-type back in 1968.

But he and Sir William always maintained that aerodynamics were the prime concern in shaping the new car and the buttresses were intended to be functional – Doug Thorpe, director of styling at Jaguar during the 1970s and early '80s,

Various XJ-S design features can be seen in sports saloon styling bucks created by Sir William in the early 1960s. Behind the scenes, updated versions of the E-type were also produced, but the XJ-S supplanted them.

Jaguar rejected a mid-engine layout for practical reasons, though Malcolm Sayer produced some scale models. But the XJ-S bears an aerodynamic relationship with the XJ13, the similarities being particularly noticeable in plan view.

This purely conjectural E-type-based styling exercise of the mid-1960s showed how the flying buttress approach was present early on in Jaguar's thinking.

recalls how Sayer explained to him that their 'twist' as they met the rear wings, unique to the XJ-S, were for an intentional aerodynamic spillage effect.

For its time the car was indeed creditably 'aerodynamic', and while at 19.8sq ft its frontal area was greater than the E-type's 17.5sq ft, its drag factor was better at .38 against the sleeker-looking 2-plus-2 E-type's .44.

Tragically, Malcolm Sayer died in 1970, though by this time the basic design and structure of the bodyshell had been finalized; Doug Thorpe didn't entirely agree with some of the car's features, including the flying buttresses, but it was too late for major changes, and only detail aspects of the design could be influenced (the biggest post-Sayer change was the adoption of a small front spoiler under the car's chin; this lowered front-end lift by 40% and moved the centre of pressure back, improving stability. That it also improved the drag factor by 6% and helped cooling were in the nature of bonuses).

So while the involuntary transfer of styling responsibility from Sayer to his successors might provide some substance to the 'designed by committee' taunt occasionally levelled at the XJ-S, in reality the styling was as much a definitive Sayer statement as the D-type or E-type had been.

Some design aspects were influenced by the legislative requirements of the North American market – one of the reasons for the demise of the E-type, the fuel tank of which could not have met the Federal 30mph rear-impact test scheduled for 1976. The XJ-S had its tank positioned across the rear suspension, well out of harm's way. Heavy, American-made piston-type Menasco struts filled with silicon rubber powder carried front and rear bumpers made from deformable plastic, to meet the US's 5mph no-damage impact test (unlike on the saloons, this arrangement was standard on home-market cars as well, and it was very effective).

Although XJ saloon-based, much less than planned of the original structure was used and finally only the front floor panels and the forward transmission tunnel were common. The shorter wheelbase was achieved by moving the rear suspension assembly – and thus the rear bulkhead – forwards, while at the front the shell was stiffened by increasing the

The XJ-S's buttresses flowed from roof down into the rear wings, turning inwards as they met the tail for an intentional air spillage effect.

triangulation of the front bulkhead and engine bay sides up to where they met the windscreen pillars.

As expected, the shorter car was torsionally stiffer than the saloon, though because of the strong rear quarters the roof contributed more strength than normal. This resulted in less shudder than in the saloon, but some extra noise and harshness had to be engineered out. Total weight of the XJ-S shell was 720lb, a useful 100lb less than the long-wheelbase saloon's.

The XJ-S incorporated everything Jaguar (and in particular Bob Knight, who had succeeded the legendary Bill Heynes as head of Jaguar's engineering) had learned about noise suppression. So besides the XJ's subframe-mounted suspension, the engine bay was shaped to deflect noise from the interior, and the front bulkhead used the same built-in

plug-and-socket electrical connections as the saloons to avoid grommeted holes. Extensive use was made of sound-deadening materials, and even such as the alloy drain tube for the air intake plenum chamber was broken by rubber sections to avoid transmitting engine and road noise.

The XJ-S used the same basic front and rear suspension assemblies as the saloon, the difference of 2cwt in weight being compensated for by bringing the spring rates down from 92 to 90lb/in at the front and from 154 to 125lb/in at the rear. Unique to the XJ-S was the rear anti-roll bar (of 0.562in diameter) fitted to increase roll stiffness; at the front, the latest specification XJ12 anti-roll bar was featured (slightly thicker than before), but at 3.5 degrees the castor angle was a degree more than the XJ12 Series 2 injection saloon's.

Sayer's original design set the bonnet line even lower, but it had to be raised to clear the engine; years later the discreet centre 'power bulge' would be enlarged to help clearance with another new engine.

The aim was to maintain a supremely good ride (even more important now that XJ27 was not simply to be a sportscar), yet provide the XJ-S driver with slightly more sporting handling. Steering was sharpened with harder rack mounting bushes and a higher ratio pinion.

Brakes were as for the XJ saloon, namely 11.18in ventilated discs with four-piston calipers at the front, and 10.38in plain inboard discs at the rear. Wheels were XJ12 alloy-type, fitted with a new steel-braced Dunlop radial tyre designated the Formula 70 SP Super Sport; still 205-section, it was claimed to provide even better wet-road grip and improved traction.

The magnificent V12 light-alloy engine was to the latest fuel-injected XJ12 specification and gave around 287bhp – like the XK 120 in its day, giving the car a useful power advantage over most contemporary American V8s. It drove through a Borg-Warner Model 12 automatic gearbox, though to the delight of the few enthusiasts who ordered one, the

Post-Sayer, detailing such as the front and rear lights exercised Doug Thorpe's styling department, and these treatments, dated September 1973, show two of many that didn't make it to production.

The XJ-S bodyshell ended up sharing less components with the XJ6 than had been intended; finally, only the forward transmission tunnel and front floorpans were common. Note the intrusion bars in the doors.

The rear end contained a platform over the rear suspension which carried a single fuel tank (unlike the two side tanks of the XJ6). Very strong, the XJ-S bodyshell's rigidity was measured as 6,460lb ft/deg unglazed, as against 4,230 for the saloon.

XJ-S was also available with the E-type's four-speed all-synchromesh manual gearbox, suitably modified to take the additional torque.

In either case, the power went to the road wheels via a Salisbury final-drive unit incorporating a 3.07:1 Powr-Lok differential. No overdrive could cope with the V12's power, but Jaguar were in the throes of developing an electrically-controlled two-speed axle – and in the impressive bank of warning lights on the dash a slot was left empty for it…almost in perpetuity for the two-speed axle was never adopted.

The interior of the XJ-S represented something of a surprise to anyone expecting XJ saloon-type appointments. Here, at least, Jaguar had continued one of their sportscar traditions – established with the XK 150 in 1957 – of abolishing wood veneer in their sporting model. Thus the XJ-S was given a vacuum-formed plastic facia in black, a black instrument panel and all-vinyl door trims. Connolly hide on the seats and thick-pile carpeting did little to offset the rather sombre, even

Carrying the front suspension and steering on a fabricated beam rubber-mounted to the body had been a Jaguar practice since 1955. For the XJ-S the arrangement was almost identical to the XJ12's. Note the ventilated discs.

Most of the car's major styling features had been finalized by the time of this styling buck. Now it was the turn of the production engineers.

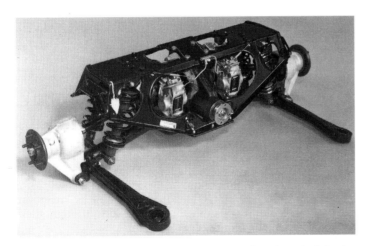

The XJ-S's subframe-mounted rear suspension, in principle the E-type/Mk 10's of 1961, used twin-coil-spring/damper units each side, aluminium hub-carriers and inboard disc brakes.

austere, look, especially when black upholstery was specified.

The XJ-S was very definitely orientated towards luxury: air conditioning was standard, as were electric windows, central locking, a radio and even five separate interior lights. It was very much a 'total package' designed to take over in many respects the flagship role from the XJ12 as the top Jaguar – perhaps not quite the original intention back in 1970. However, when plans for an open version (coded XJ28) had to be dropped, refinement and comfort gradually usurped outright sporting appeal as the main design priority, and it is probably true to say that the XJ-S's character underwent a definite change of emphasis between prototype and production stages.

CHAPTER 2

A V12 express

The first production XJ-S

Jaguar had developed a magnificent new GT car, but it was yet to be named. Some argued that the C/D/E sequence should be continued, giving F-type or XK-F. Others argued for Jaguar Le Mans, but that designation was already in use on a Pontiac (which, like the XJ-S, had never been anywhere near Le Mans!). Eventually, according to journalist John Dugdale, Jaguar's marketing director Bob Berry said: "The car is going to be called XJ dash S"; and that was that.

But how did the XJ-S impact on press and public, and how did it work on the road? Its overall performance was, in a word, superlative. The XJ-S was usefully quicker and tauter-handling than the 12-cylinder Jaguar saloons, yet retained their refinement and already legendary disdain for poor road surfaces. The XJ-S flowed rather than merely drove, wafted from corner to corner by the discreet might of its superb power unit. Where speed limits and traffic allowed, 120 to 130mph was an unflustered cruising speed, obtained in less than half-a-minute from standstill.

While by no means faultless, the XJ-S quickly proved itself to be a car which elevated the term Grand Tourer on to an altogether higher plane; deliberately pitched at an entirely different segment of the high-performance market to that of the E-type, it could challenge cars like the 450 SLC Mercedes (hence its gauntlet-throwing debut at Frankfurt) for sheer competence in long-distance, high-speed ground covering.

As Jaguar half-expected by the time of the launch, the car's styling attracted mixed reviews. Nor did the interior completely escape criticism: while the speedometer and tachometer retained the clear, white-lettering-on-black style, they were placed within rather cheap-looking cowls, and the secondary instruments monitoring water, oil, fuel and voltage were an unusual, technically-advanced vertical drum type using three opposing coils. They were quick-acting and more accurate than the normal round type, but some owners felt them to be 'un-Jaguar'.

XJ6-type stalks controlled wipers, indicators and headlight dip/flash, and while the steering wheel retained the same 15½in diameter as in the saloons, it was given a new, leather-bound rim. The XJ6's umbrella-type handbrake was swopped for one which lay outboard of the driver's seat, and which after being applied dropped down to floor level again, out of the way.

The car's seats were all-new. Sports types featured in the front, fully reclining and with a new two-section cushion having a 'soft' centre and a harder surround, providing lateral support by gently locating the occupant. Individual-style rear seats were fitted, separated by a tray (containing the rear seat belt buckles where fitted) over the propshaft tunnel; beautifully trimmed, they could accommodate two adults, but only if those in the front didn't mind pulling their seats forward quite a way. The car was thus more fairly described as a 2-plus-2 than a genuine four-seater, headroom as well as kneeroom being another limiting factor. Fine for the kids, though, making the XJ-S a true family car at a pinch.

The hard facts – plus the usual subjective opinion – were soon supplied by the motoring press. In Britain, *Autocar* found that its manual version reached 60mph in 6.9 seconds

This is what met the eyes of the press on the car's UK launch – a large but sleek car quite unlike anything seen before from Jaguar.

A new car and a new name, carried on the matt black bootlid panel. 'S', it seems, stood for Special. While referred to as a GT in Jaguar's sales literature, no such initials appeared on the XJ-S itself.

and 100mph in only 11 seconds more, and recorded a maximum of 153mph. Despite performance testing, a fuel consumption of 15.4mpg was recorded overall, and it was thought that 20mpg was within reach, given gentle driving over a longish journey – if so, fuel injection had certainly brought its benefits to the V12.

Motor were unable to carry out a maximum-speed check on their manual XJ-S, but recorded marginally better acceleration figures, 100mph arriving in 16.2 instead of 16.9 seconds. The considerably poorer figure of 12.8mpg overall and the (projected) 'touring' mpg of 14.4 which *Motor* obtained do tally more closely with those found by owners of pre-HE cars, though 16 to 17mpg was quite feasible on a long run if the driver could resist using the silky surge of acceleration at every opportunity.

Both journals considered the steering to be on the light side, but were not over-critical of it; *Motor's* testers commented on the slight tendency of the car to 'float' over undulations taken at speed – a feature of the XJ saloons, too, and due to Jaguar placing ride marginally over handling when it came to suspension settings. Otherwise, the car received the usual lavish praise for its 'exemplary' handling and 'remarkable' ride. Both magazines considered that for carrying large adults, the rear seats were for occasional use only – though *Motor* pointed out that the Aston Martin V8 and the Jensen Interceptor were equally at fault in this direction.

As indicated, both these test cars were fitted with the manual gearbox. This was a development of the four-speed all-synchromesh box introduced in 1964, and while it was reliable, by 1975 it had fallen a little behind the best; both *Motor* and *Autocar* commented on the stickiness of the change, and the former, too, on the comparative heaviness of the clutch (which needed a 38lb push). A pity, maybe, that the Jaguar-designed five-speed gearbox never made it to production.

But it was the manual transmission that enabled the smoothness, flexibility and response of the V12 engine to be savoured to the full, and *Autocar* recounted the 'top-gear starting' feat, whereby you placed the lever in top, switched on, engaged the starter, and allowed the engine to pick up and accelerate all the way to 140mph without touching the clutch – in just under 70 seconds... 'Such flexibility has been the goal of engine designers since the beginning of the internal combustion engine', said the road-test report.

Most customers specified the Model 12 automatic box. It was well suited to the smooth effortlessness of the car, but it had some shortcomings even though it was more 'sporty' than the GM unit to come, and it was no coincidence that all of Jaguar's early press road-test cars were released in manual form only. The Borg-Warner box could prove reluctant to change down, was a bit slow off the mark from standstill, and was generally lazy in the way it performed, irritatingly so to the keen driver. However, in more relaxed conditions it was perfectly adequate and it suited the majority of buyers, who were more 'executive' than 'sporting'. There were the usual first and second gear holds, but using the quadrant manually resulted in only fractions of seconds being saved on acceleration.

The XJ-S received the same rather mixed reception in the United States as it had in Europe, some considering its appearance rather too much like such home-based offerings as the Camaro, GM's response to the Mustang (actually, the XJ-S was 4in shorter and the same width as the Camaro – but

SEPTEMBER 10, 1975. A BLACK DAY FOR MODENA, STUTTGART AND TURIN.

What's good news for Britain has to be bad news for our foreign competitors.
And the best news of this or any other year has to be the Jaguar XJS.
No other car made currently offers a comparable combination of performance and luxury at anywhere near the price.
Which explains why export orders for the XJS are already expected to be in excess of £20 million. In the first year.
Needless to say, performance of the XJS is

startling. Zero to sixty takes under seven seconds. Top speed, where permissible, is in the region of 150 mph.
Yet this level of performance is achieved in levels of silence and safety that will astonish and delight you. As will the mpg figures.
Technically, the XJS has many features which are unique to Jaguar.
And the list of luxury and safety features fitted as standard equipment is long and impressive.

Which is as it should be, considering that the XJS has been designed to be the definitive Jaguar.
Which makes it, in many ways, the definitive high-performance luxury car.
September 10, 1975. A great day for British motoring. And for Britain.

The Jaguar XJS
The car everyone dreams of.
But very, very few can ever own.

With the XJ-S Jaguar attacked the exotic end of the sportscar market for the first time.

in the large expanse of bonnet and sloping roofline there were definite similarities). Likewise, the interior was sometimes a disappointment: 'pure Pinto', said *Car and Driver* with regret, hankering after the saloons' wood dashboard.

GKN alloy wheels with 6in rims relieved the more sombre touches bestowed by the black bumpers and window surrounds. The side view emphasizes the car's low build, at 4ft 2in no higher than a 2-plus-2 E-type. Note the lip spoiler at the front, quite a late addition to the design.

It was the rear end which was the most unorthodox, while the detailing of the side window vents was the subject of some discussion. Whatever its styling, the car performed superbly on the road.

Many at Jaguar had doubts about the flying buttresses – one last-minute suggestion was to fair them in with a cover similar to XJ-13's, an idea rejected by Sir William. At least the aerodynamics kept the shallow rear screen clean when it rained!

The original XJ-S with its chief progenitors – the Series 3 E-type which first used the V12 engine, and the XJ12 (this being the contemporary Series 2 coupe) which provided the chassis.

Easily the roomiest 2-plus-2 Jaguar to date, the XJ-S's seats were wide, yet still sporting. They alone were trimmed in leather (or optionally velour), vinyls and plastics dominating the rest of the interior.

The very modern instrument binnacle contained new 'air core' barrel-type secondary instruments sandwiched by a 160mph speedometer and a tachometer red-lined at 6,500rpm. Above were a row of warning lights monitoring many different functions – note the blank one, third from the right, which had been intended for the two-speed axle (if lit, it actually reads 'overdrive').

Until 1979 the XJ-S could be bought with a four-speed manual transmission with a traditional gear lever – as this young lady is pointing out in this publicity shot.

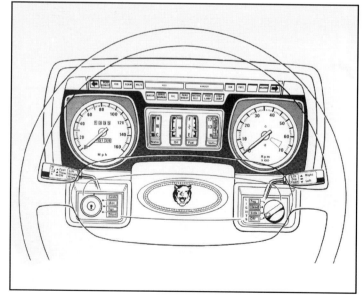

Everyone acknowledged the car's ability, though. 'It's more than a little eerie', recounted *Road Test* magazine, almost in awe. 'It never ruffled its feathers, never tried to turn around and snap. It just flexed its broad shoulders and worked.' Or, as Patrick Bedard wrote in *Car and Driver*: 'The XJ-S is a dark and mysterious product of England's tortured auto industry, fantastically over-qualified for today's driving conditions…'

The boot was almost as deep as it was wide and took a perfectly adequate amount of luggage; battery and upright spare wheel were protected by neat covers. The 20-gallon petrol tank sat across the rear axle.

Beautifully trimmed, with perforated leather for the fluting, the rear seats were suitable only for two adults over short journeys, but they were excellent for children.

Cars destined for North America looked very similar to their European-market kin, except for their four separate GEC tungsten headlights instead of the advanced and highly efficient Cibie streamlined halogen units. Opinions vary as to which was visually better; as a design exercise, a European four-headlight version using Cibie 5¾in units was later produced by Jaguar experimentally, but it was not well received by the management and it was many years before 'proper' headlights were seen on a UK-market XJ-S.

More seriously, perhaps, detoxing equipment under the bonnet took its toll on brake horsepower; Federal cars had exhaust gas recirculation, an anti-run-on valve, an evaporative emissions carbon canister for the fuel tank, and a catalytic converter serving each bank of cylinders. Power went down to 244bhp at 5,250rpm and the 40bhp drop affected acceleration to 60mph by around a second, and to 100mph by nearer 4 seconds, despite a lower (3.31:1) final-drive ratio. Economy wasn't helped by all this, either, and this was to contribute towards an early crisis for the XJ-S – which nearly didn't make it very far into the 1980s.

The heart of the XJ-S was its magnificent 5.3-litre (326cu in) engine with Lucas/Bosch electronic fuel injection and Lucas Opus Mk II ignition system – though with fuel rails and air conditioning plumbing it all looks very busy! Note the bracing struts from bulkhead to inner wings, and the brake servo bottom right.

The XJ-S for the North American market had to carry lower-wattage, round headlamps of a more orthodox type than the advanced Cibie units fitted for the UK and many other markets.

CHAPTER 3

Egan and the HE save the XJ-S

May cylinder head brings performance with economy

Early on in its career the XJ-S changed less visually year-to-year than the Jaguar saloons, partly because (as Doug Thorpe once pointed out) the overall shape of the car did not easily lend itself to a major facelift, and partly because of Jaguar's straightforward lack of money and resources. So the first changes, in 1977, did not affect the XJ-S's appearance much. Most significant was the substitution in April of the GM 400 gearbox for the Borg-Warner Model 12. This was more responsive, though it still left an annoying 'performance gap' around 35 to 50mph as it still refused to reselect first gear once on the move, either by kick-down or manually.

Cosmetic changes arrived in the autumn of 1977 with the 1978-model XJ-S swopping its black-finished radiator grille for a bright-finished one; black was also replaced on the bootlid's rear panel by body-colour. The central door pillar, however, adopted a matt-black finish, and inside, the instrument bezels lost their silver surrounds.

The year 1979 was notable mostly for the demise of the manual gearbox option for the XJ-S. Demand was simply not high enough to justify retaining it and midway during the year the four-speeder was dropped from the range; for the record, the last production manual XJ-S was finished in Squadron Blue and carried the VIN number JNAEW1 AC 101814, though it is believed that at least two further manual XJ-Ss were completed to special order afterwards. But early attempts were made to brighten the interior with twin-colour console and better quality carpeting.

During 1979 and 1980 the XJ-S was rather overshadowed by the new Series 3 saloons, and there was no distinct 1980 model as such. Instead, further efforts were made to improve economy pending the introduction of the radical new May cylinder heads. Meanwhile, having suffered under a British Leyland management unable to appreciate the uniqueness of Jaguar, the company finally found a saviour in the form of John Egan, who was appointed in April 1980 by BL boss Michael Edwardes to "sort out Jaguar or it will be closed". That Egan succeeded in his task is now a matter of history, but at the time nothing was certain.

The mid-1980 interim changes centred around the adoption of the latest Lucas/Bosch digital electronic fuel injection and a rise in compression ratio to 10:1, which in practice decreased fuel consumption by a couple of mpg overall. They also increased the power to 300bhp at 5,400rpm and peak torque to 318lb ft at 3,900rpm.

In the United States, the improvement was even more marked, thanks to the substitution of a three-way converter for the previous air injection and exhaust gas recirculation emissions gear; this raised US-specification cars from 244 to 262bhp, which helped to knock a whole second off the 0–60mph time (now 7.8 seconds) despite a 3.07:1 instead of a 3.31:1 final-drive ratio. Fuel consumption dropped from around 12mpg to nearer 14mpg in normal driving conditions. These pre-HE 'digital' cars were remarkably quick, but were in production for a matter of months only, making them a sub-model of some rarity.

The next, and considerably more significant, update took place in July 1981 – and it was certainly needed because in the years since the car's launch sales had slumped, produc-

Prior to the HE of 1981, the XJ-S's appearance changed little except for a bright-finished radiator grille, a black centre door pillar and body-colour on the bootlid rear panel for 1978.

In North America the twin-headlight car, with its less powerful, 'emissions' engine – and a less than ideal reliability record – was making slow progress in the sales charts, but this pre-HE car gave the model a boost when it 'won' the coast-to-coast Cannonball run in 1983, finishing ahead of both US and German-built rivals.

July 1981 saw the launch of the highly significant HE model. Apart from badging, it was externally identified by new 6½in-rim 'starfish' alloy wheels, twin coachlines and bright plated bumper cappings, while the scuttle air intake grille was now black. All cars now adopted indicator repeater lights in the front wings.

The badge of success: the all-important HE initials, which heralded a new era for the XJ-S and a new lease of life for the V12 engine.

tion falling from a peak of 3,890 in 1977 to just 1,057 in 1980, when Jaguar's American market went into something of a depression. All large, thirsty and expensive cars suffered, and Jaguar even contemplated discontinuing the V12 engine – with plans being drawn up for an XK-powered interim XJ-S. Nor were XJ-S sales helped by the car's poor reliability record and its high price, especially on the North American market (the XJ12 actually had to be withdrawn altogether).

However, Michael May represented the cavalry on this occasion, along with John Egan's quality campaign and a realization that more traditional Jaguar appointments had to be built into the car. May, an independent Swiss engineer, had circulated his ideas on what came to be known as the 'fireball' combustion chamber to the industry in 1976, and it wasn't long before Jaguar's power units division, then headed by Harry Mundy, saw the possibilities of applying it to the V12. So a contract was signed.

Basically, the May combustion chamber is a split-level arrangement giving a low-turbulence, concentrated charge round the sparking plug, which enables rapid and complete

25

Cutaway HE engine showing the chamber around the inlet valve and the flat pistons. Also revealed are the duplex timing chains driving the single cam per bank, and the typical Jaguar bucket tappets.

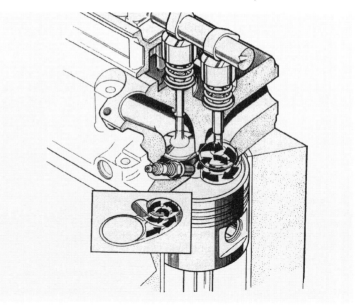

This diagram illustrates the principles of the May head, with the compression stroke introducing a swirl in the fireball combustion chamber; inset, shows the underside of the swirl pattern.

burning of very lean mixtures to take place under a very high compression ratio. Of course, in simple terms, the leaner the mixture and the higher the compression ratio, the more efficient the engine.

A 12.5:1 compression was used with a new high-power amplifier, twin-coil system to provide the 100% greater ignition energy required. As the mixture combustion now took place in the cylinder head, flat-topped pistons replaced the dished type, and the latest-type Lucas digital electronic fuel injection was reprogrammed to suit the new lean-burn characteristics of the engine, which was named the HE, standing for High Efficiency. With the announcement of the HE range on July 15, 1981, Jaguar were the first to get the May system in production. The results were well worth the effort – and the £½-million expense – of modifying the cylinder head plant at Radford to machine the new combustion chambers into the previously 'flat' heads.

While economy had been the main aim, extra efficiency meant extra power, too, and this enabled Jaguar to raise the final-drive ratio to 2.88:1, further helping economy and pushing the top speed to around 155mph. But more importantly,

steady-speed fuel consumption improved dramatically: on the official urban cycle the HE gave (with previous figures in brackets) 15.6mpg (12.7), at 56mph 27.1 (21.9), and at 75mph 22.5 (18.6). In practice this made 20mpg a real proposition for an XJ-S, a figure of great psychological importance!

Motor tested an XJ-S HE in October 1981 and confirmed the improvement – the latest car was 21% more economical at 16.3mpg overall than their previous road-test XJ-S, this figure including performance-testing. The journal also commented that 'it is now possible to achieve an astounding 22mpg at an average (over 650 miles) of more than 62mph' – which required driving the XJ-S at 80mph whenever possible.

It was a pity that some of these benefits were lost on US-specification cars, which carried four catalyst converters. A Federal XJ-S would typically return as little as 10mpg during fast driving, and there was a fairly drastic performance penalty as well, 0–100mph taking around 21 seconds as opposed to 17 seconds for the European example.

Customer feedback, especially in the States, clearly indicated

The HE's new interior was just as vital as the May-head engine, giving the car traditional Jaguar furnishings in the form of wood veneers and extensive real leather trim.

The man who realized what the potential XJ-S customer wanted, and then provided it with the XJ-S HE – John Egan, later knighted for his services to British exports. Here he presents rising star Nigel Mansell with the keys to his new black and gold HE at Browns Lane in the spring of 1982.

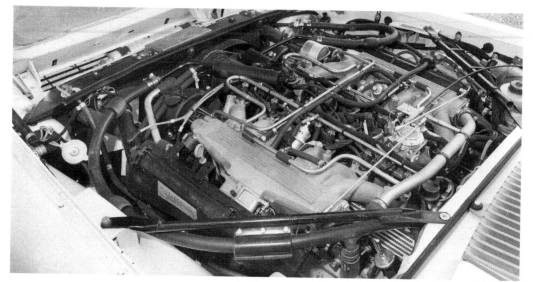

XJ-S engine evolution. Development stages are best identified by the fuel rails: this very early (1975) power unit has the twin-routed round-section rails overlapping the induction manifolding, as used for the first five years. Note the amplifier unit (needed to adapt the Bosch D Jetronic injection system to 12 cylinders) mounted over the radiator.

The comparatively rare Lucas/ Bosch digital injection engine which appeared during 1980. There is a now a single-routed, round-section fuel rail, while the amplifier has gone from on top of the radiator. This is an LHD 'emissions' engine.

An early 1981 HE engine with single round-section fuel rail; note the 'black box' mounted above the left-hand bank, part of the new high-power ignition system required for the 12.5:1 compression ratio May heads.

Later HE engines (this is a 1988-model car photographed in October 1987) had revised, square-section fuel rails, installed after reports of leaks. Most earlier HE engines have been fitted with these square-section rails retrospectively.

The 1983-model XJ-S HE, shortly before being updated for 1984 with headlamp wash/wipe and other goodies. Note the 'antique'-finish bonnet badge.

that the XJ-S was regarded more as a luxury sports coupe than a sportscar. So at last the XJ-S was trimmed like a true Jaguar, with real leather replacing vinyl on the door casings, centre console and rear-quarter trim panels, while – above all – hand-crafted wood veneer appeared on the facia, centre switch panel and door cappings. These improvements enriched the whole interior of the car and transformed its market appeal.

The opportunity was also taken to adopt some Series 3 modernizations – a new leather-bound Series 3-type steering wheel, revised instrument and switch graphics, a delay wipe facility (and revised wiper blade operation to clear a greater area of the screen), improved electric window switches, a timer-linked rear window heater element, a courtesy light delay (plus red guard lamps in the door pockets to provide a 'door open' warning), an improved central locking system to allow both doors to be locked by either of the exterior or interior locks on each door (the centre console door lock switch was deleted) and a new range of interior trim colours. In the boot, a Series 3-type courtesy light was fitted.

Outside, the HE sported new dome-type 'starfish' alloy wheels with a 6½-inch rim width and a jaguar head in the centre, 215 section Dunlop D7 tyres or Pirelli P5, a tapering twin coachline along the length of the body, Series 3-type plated-top bumpers, US-style side repeater lights and black-finished scuttle-mounted heater/air-conditioner intakes and wiper arms. The all-important 'HE' symbol appeared on the left-hand side of the bootlid, and a new antique-finish medallion embossed with the jaguar head (vaguely reminiscent of the original XK 120 badge) featured on the bonnet.

Helped by the combination of better fuel economy, greater reliability, more traditional appointments and (in the United States) a 24-month/36,000-mile warranty, the XJ-S quickly became a best-seller at home and abroad. By 1982 annual production was up to 3,455, and in 1984 the 5,000 mark was shattered with a total of 5,814 cars being made.

But Jaguar, and John Egan in particular, were intent on widening the car's appeal still further, and the next major change to the XJ-S was eventually to result in record-breaking sales.

CHAPTER 4

The 3.6-litre and Cabriolets

AJ6 engine brings a sportier image

In October 1983 a six-cylinder XJ-S arrived with an entirely new powertrain, including a new Jaguar engine – the first since the V12 of 1971. The result was a lighter, sportier XJ-S with improved economy and the advantage (to the enthusiast driver) of a five-speed manual gearbox – standard in this, the new XJ-S 3.6. Also, there was now an open Jaguar again, for the familiar coupe was being joined by a cabriolet body style.

The XJ-S 3.6 also gave Jaguar a useful low-volume trial period for the new AJ6 (Advanced Jaguar Six) power unit, which was scheduled to replace the revered XK engine as Jaguar's mainstream saloon power unit. Its use in the XJ-S was very much akin to Jaguar offering the first XK engine in the XK 120 and the V12 engine in the E-type prior to either of these being seen in saloon cars. This period of grace was to prove vital in the development of the AJ6 unit.

The 3,590cc, 91 x 92mm, twin-overhead-camshaft, all-aluminium AJ6 engine, the basic design features of which had been laid out by Harry Mundy, had emerged in its final form only after exploratory exercises centred around straight-six, V6 and V8 variations of the 12-cylinder engine and 24-valve versions of the faithful XK engine. Finally, a completely new design was decided upon featuring an aluminium block which continued well below the centreline of the seven-main-bearing crankshaft and used interference-fit dry liners. Initially, it used a cast-iron crankshaft (which was easier and cheaper to manufacture than Jaguar's traditional forged variety) and carried an up-to-the-minute four-valves-per-cylinder aluminium head, this valve arrangement giving excellent breathing and lower mechanical stresses. Jaguar

stuck to chains for operating the twin overhead camshafts.

Lucas/Bosch P digital fuel injection was used and a 9.6:1 compression ratio was chosen; this gave 225bhp at 5,300rpm and 240lb ft of torque at 4,000rpm, which compared very favourably with the fuel-injected 4.2 XK unit's 205bhp at 5,000rpm and 236lb ft of torque at 3,750rpm – or the 5.3 engine's 299/318 figures, too, for that matter. Also, one of the XK engine's biggest disadvantages had been overcome – its weight. The new engine scaled 430lb, compared with 553lb for the XK, both in test-bed condition (the V12 weighed 640lb).

The first prototype AJ6-engined XJ-S (coded XJ57) was running by the spring of 1980, originally with what was termed the 2000-series block, a 3.8-litre sand-cast open-deck unit with wet liners; the 3000-series closed-deck block with its dry liners superseded it, and a 3.8-litre version remained in the running for a while until it was decided that the 3.6-litre engine provided all the power and torque necessary.

Jaguar's XJ57 project engineer Paul Walker admitted that substituting 3.6 litres for 5.3 litres represented a challenge if performance was to be maintained; the long inlet tracts are partly evidence of the need to produce as much low and mid-range torque as possible.

Chassis changes to the car were few, just softer front springs (reduced from 423 to 329lb/in) and the deletion of the rear anti-roll bar. This would normally tend to increase understeer, but the right balance was obtained due to the reduction of front-end weight courtesy of the AJ6 engine. Wheels were a perforated alloy type soon nicknamed 'pepperpots'.

The 3.6 XJ-S Coupe brought a brand new engine to the Jaguar range and, with its greater economy and sporting character, also attracted a new sort of customer. But the V12 coupe remained the most popular XJS, outselling the 'six' by a large margin until the 4.0 litre arrived.

Externally, the 3.6 Coupe differed little from the HE except for the 3.6 badge and 'pepperpot' Series 3-type alloy wheels. The model was excellent value at £19,248, being £2,504 cheaper than the V12.

Jaguar amazed other manufacturers by their ability to produce the world's first mass-production, all-aluminium, dohc 24-valve engine. Machined alloy cam covers featured, with a stainless-steel cover decorously shielding the exhaust manifolding.

The 225bhp injected engine was canted over to allow room for longer than usual inlet tracts, these helping to increase torque.

The 3.6 Coupe owner enjoyed leather upholstery and shiny wood veneers; however, the original instrument binnacle, with barrel minor instruments, remained. This is an early, 1984 model year, car.

The Getrag five-speed gearbox did much to give the 3.6 a sporting feel. Incidentally, except for a batch of 25 shipped there in 1984 to assess customer and dealer reaction, no 3.6 manual cars went to the US.

The castor angle remained the same (it had been discreetly changed from 2.5 to 3.5 degrees about two years previously to crispen response a little), but a slightly stiffer torsion bar was used in the power steering, giving a little more driver effort. The aim was to produce a slightly more sporting feel, yet without interfering with the XJ-S's famed handling/ride balance.

Jaguar succeeded in this, *Motor* commenting on the car's improved turn-in characteristics (even if the damping still allowed a certain amount of float over undulations taken at speed); *Autocar* also appreciated 'a welcome improvement in response'. Performance compared with the V12-engined car had really suffered very little – *Autocar* found their Coupe reached a mean 141mph and, at 6.7 seconds, equalled the former's 0–60mph time. The time to 100mph was 19.7 seconds, which was 4 seconds down on the HE and about the same as a 4.2 litre 2-plus-2 E-type.

Of course, the new manual transmission helped and, together with the slightly tauter handling, the new Getrag five-speed gearbox made the XJ-S into much more of a real sportscar – the driver could now select exactly the right ratio for any given road condition. So on all but motorways the new 3.6 was as quick as the 5.3 – and a good deal more economical, giving some 17.5mpg when driven fast and 22–24mpg with gentler use.

Not that the AJ6 engine's installation was a total success, for these early AJ6 units left something to be desired in respect of refinement. Also, the Getrag five-speed gearbox was found on occasion to be a little obstructive, its five-plane gate was awkward, and the rather heavy clutch needed to be depressed fully to produce a baulk-free change. Though soon cured by reprogramming the ECU, the overrun fuel cut-off contributed some jerkiness when the injection system re-introduced mixture at 800rpm.

The advanced ZF automatic gearbox, as used on the latest BMWs, was originally scheduled for the 3.6, but as the installation was taking longer than expected to develop, Jaguar opted for the simpler Getrag manual box. The existing Jaguar/Rover '77mm' manual box, as seen on a few Series 3 saloons, wasn't used, incidentally, because it was already at its engine-torque limit.

The luggage bay of an early 3.6 Coupe; the fire extinguisher was a factory option.

The 'OK for kids' rear seats continued as before in the 3.6 Coupe.

The Cabriolet

Two models with the new engine were offered: the XJ-S 3.6 Coupe, which retained the original XJ-S profile, and the XJ-SC 3.6, with its attention-getting cabriolet roof. Jaguar now offered an open two-seater again for the first time since the E-type left the new-car lists in 1975. A convertible XJ-S had been projected much earlier, and had even received a code name (XJ28), but lack of money and the general depression which enveloped the XJ-S had prevented it becoming a serious proposition.

However, when John Egan arrived at Jaguar in 1980 the atmosphere changed and within months an open XJ-S was created. The cabriolet approach, using a centre bracing hoop, was chosen as there was not enough funding to modify and strengthen the bodyshell for a proper convertible – or to carry rear seats, which was the major reason why the new variant was a two-seater, with lockable storage boxes featuring in lieu of rear seats.

The build procedure for the new Cabriolet was somewhat involved. The XJ-SC started life as a standard XJ-S bodyshell at the Castle Bromwich works, except for the omission of the roof and rear header panel; Park Sheet Metal then fitted a new rear deck panel (having removed those buttresses!), strengthened the floorpan through additional stiffening of the transmission tunnel and a new crossmember under the rear suspension unit, and installed the centre crossbar – which incorporated one of the two tubular steel roll-over bars extending down to sill level (the other was contained within the cant-rails over the door apertures).

The shell then travelled back to Castle Bromwich for painting, then went on to Browns Lane for the installation of mechanical components and trim. The tailoring and installation of the Targa-type hood was carried out by Aston Martin Tickford, after which the car rejoined the XJ-S line and underwent road-testing and a quality audit before being despatched to a dealer.

An entirely new Cabriolet body style was launched alongside the 3.6 Coupe. This example has HE-type 'starfish' alloy wheels.

Not entirely open, the Cabriolet retained a perimeter roof frame and a crossbar to preserve rigidity. The integral rear top folded away beneath an envelope.

The V12 Cabriolet arrived in July 1985. This shows the car in completely closed condition.

The open-top arrangements allowed the driver quite a choice. There were two fabric-covered interlocking panels making up the detachable roof (when not erected these could be placed in a storage envelope carried in the boot), a 'half-hardtop' made from double-skinned GRP and carrying a built-in heated rear window, and finally a rear hood with its own window, which could be erected instead of the hardtop. When lowered, the hood stowed away below the rear deck-line, folded under a padded cover. Thus almost saloon-car comfort and silence could be enjoyed with the rigid panels in place, or semi-open-air sportscar motoring with them removed and the rear hood down.

The new models certainly emphasized the revival in the fortunes of the XJ-S, which had been evident from the moment the HE model had been introduced. Demand for the 3.6-litre cars was high, but as production volumes were low, a waiting list for them soon developed, despite the fact that they had been priced somewhat higher than some people expected – £19,248 for the Coupe and £20,756 for the Cabriolet, the latter being only £1,000 less than the XJ-S HE.

Still, the majority of rivals remained considerably more expensive – the nearest equivalent Mercedes-Benz was now the 380 SEC, which cost £29,930, the BMW 635CSi was £24,995, and the Porsche 928S Series 2 cost £30,679. Of the whole bunch, *Autocar* reckoned that despite its known shortcomings, the 3.6 Jaguar 'so clearly offers the best blend of qualities for the price; superb noise refinement and ride, with good handling, largely effortless performance, competitive levels of economy for the class, and air conditioning... it remains a hard act for the others to follow'.

HE developments

Rather overshadowed by the launch of the dashing Cabriolet and the exciting new engine, the XJ-S HE nevertheless continued as the ultimate high-performance Jaguar, and for 1984 several further refinements were added – an improved stereo radio/cassette with digital tuning, a trip computer, cruise control and headlamp wash/wipe, all of which were extras on the 3.6.

This made the car better value than ever; those used to

The interior of the XJ-SC HE, viewed through the open roof.

forking out hundreds – or even thousands – of pounds or dollars for additional equipment on other prestige makes, almost as a matter of course, found the simple statement in Jaguar's XJ-S HE catalogue: 'Optional extras: none', particularly impressive. The HE now cost £21,750, which made it highly competitive against the Mercedes 500 SEC at £30,375, for example.

A V12 Cabriolet

Ironically, the very model which looked like becoming the first casualty in the XJ range was becoming one of the strongest sellers; in 1984 the XJ-S sold a record worldwide total of 6,028 units, 3,480 of them in the United States. The appeal of the car was further broadened when, on July 17, 1985, Jaguar announced a V12-engined Cabriolet to accompany the six-cylinder version. This brought the mainstream XJ-S range up to four models: 3.6 or 5.3-litre Coupe and 3.6 or 5.3-litre Cabriolet.

The new model immediately became one of the world's

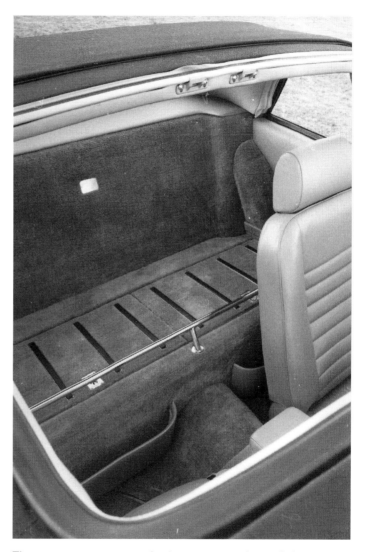

There were no rear seats in the open cars; instead there was a carpeted luggage platform with opening lockers big enough to take a small briefcase.

Rear badging described the Cabriolet thus; on the other side of the number-plate there would be HE for the V12 or 3.6 for the smaller-engined model.

The quite heavy roof panels, difficult for slightly-built ladies to handle, were stowed in this bag in the boot, all part of a rather involved procedure which, while tolerated by the British, tended to cause amazement amongst Americans used to one-touch 'power' folding tops!

The 'pull down and turn' locking handles for the two detachable roof panels.

fastest open cars, thanks to its 295bhp May-headed V12 engine (and despite retaining the three-speed automatic gearbox). Tyres were 215/70 VR15 on 'Starfish' 6.5J cast-alloy wheels. A limited-slip Powr-Lok differential was standard and, like the AJ6-engined Cabriolet, the car was a two-seater. Weather equipment and interior trim followed the 3.6 Cabriolet's with elm veneer and all-leather treatment of seats, door panels and centre console. Air conditioning was standard, as were a trip computer, cruise control, electrically adjustable door mirrors and a Clarion E950 stereo.

The V12 Cabriolet was identified externally by XJ-SC HE badging on the bootlid and a V12 motif on the radiator grille. The paint was augmented by twin coachlines.

Demand had outstripped supply ever since the first Cabriolet had been announced in the autumn of 1983, and to speed up the build of the car, from the introduction of the V12

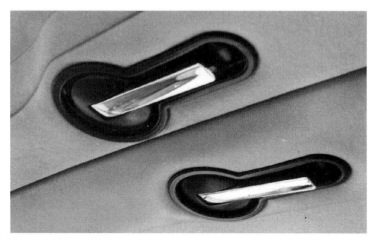

Wash/wipe became standard on the HE for 1984, but remained an extra on the 3.6 cars.

Cabriolet the new roof was fitted entirely 'in house'. It was still quite an expensive car, however, at £26,995 in the UK.

The Cabriolets were handsome and reasonably practical cars, even if the twin interlocking roof panels (removable together or singly) were a little cumbersome to manhandle and not always watertight. This writer recalls that there could be quite severe buffeting at around 70mph with the car open, but the shell's rigidity was acceptable and, with the roof on, wind noise was only slightly worse than in the Coupe. Though always a low-volume seller, mainly due to the complex build procedure, the model quickly found its adherents and many enthusiasts admire the Cabriolet today.

The new model made its British show debut at Motorfair in September 1985 – 50 years to the month after the original Jaguar range was launched in London. Alongside was a mildly revised V12 Coupe in which burr walnut replaced burr elm, while the letters 'HE' were dropped from the badging, which became simply V12 XJ-S. The 3.6 Coupe retained burr elm veneer, but sported plusher carpets and seats with more luxurious new wool trim facings set in stitched leather surrounds. However, the two 3.6-litre variants were still available only with the five-speed manual transmission. Finally, to celebrate the racing victories of the TWR team's XJ-Ss in Europe, British Racing Green returned to Jaguar's colour charts!

CHAPTER 5

The Convertible alternative

Plus a handling pack brings more sporting appeal

North America did not receive the Cabriolet until April 1986, and then only in V12 5.3-litre, 262bhp 'emissions' form; for a specialist model it was received well, 575 being sold in its inaugural year and 1,015 in 1987. Yet Jaguar Cars Inc considered that its customers, used to power-top full convertibles, would not easily accept the somewhat do-it-yourself roof arrangements (the 'erector-set car' as some called it) and, with the encouragement of the dealerships, decided to augment this 'official' open model with one of their own until such time as a proper Jaguar convertible appeared.

Hess & Eisenhardt

The Jaguar XJ-S Convertible by Hess & Eisenhardt was announced by Jaguar's Leonia, New Jersey headquarters on October 29, 1986 and it became available on special order through US Jaguar dealers almost immediately. Hess & Eisenhardt, based in Cincinnati, Ohio and founded in 1876, were rated as one of America's leading coachbuilders and had long built convertibles on Cadillac and Buick chassis.

They were given an 18-month contract by Jaguar Cars Inc to produce a two-seater convertible from a complete, standard XJ-S V12 Coupe. The interior was stripped, the body placed on a jig, and steel structural members welded to the main sills before the roof and rear quarter panels were removed. New panels were welded in before the top part of the car was repainted, blending in with the untouched bottom half.

The full electrically operated top was designed to fold deeply into the body where, concealed under a colour co-ordinated cover, it would disturb the car's smooth lines only minimally. However, this meant exchanging the single fuel tank for two, an upper tank feeding into a lower one. Unfortunately, although the initially leak-prone connection was eventually made fuel-tight, the car always seemed to smell of petrol, and it was also a battle to maintain quality, a common enough hazard with a low-volume specialist model.

Mechanically, the car was identical to the V12 Coupe and, covered by a 36-month, 36,000-mile warranty, its recommended retail price was $47,000. Though it certainly had failings, the Hess & Eisenhardt Convertible served to fill the gap until Jaguar's own full convertible could be put into production.

Automatic transmission for the 3.6

In February 1987, both the 3.6-litre Coupe and Cabriolet were finally given the option of automatic transmission, thanks largely to the development programme which had been put in hand for the all-new XJ6 (XJ40) saloon launched the previous year.

The four-speed ZF 4HP 22 transmission, carefully matched to the 3.6-litre engine, was essentially a three-speed epicyclic box with third gear equating to direct drive; fourth was an 'overdrive' ratio for optimum economy, this aspect also being enhanced by a lock-up clutch operating within the torque converter on top gear. The selector was a conventional one, the so-called 'Randle Handle' (nicknamed after Jim Randle, Jaguar's engineering chief at the time), with its U-shaped two-branch lever position, remaining exclusive to the saloon.

The Hess & Eisenhardt Convertible, commissioned by Jaguar Cars Inc in the USA during 1986 (this is a 1988 model). Considerable efforts were made to avoid a high, Germanic-looking folded top, but the stock windscreen looked clumsy compared with Jaguar's own Convertible when that appeared in March 1988.

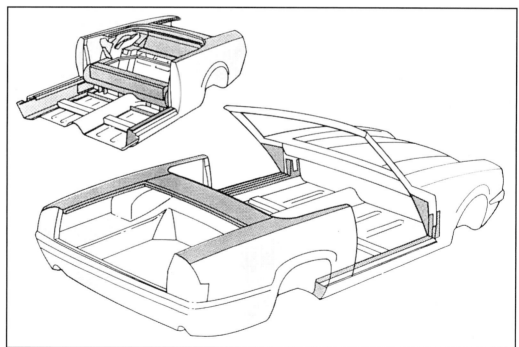

The shaded areas on this diagram show the new or modified panels of the Hess & Eisenhardt Convertible, including the new rear tonneau panel, lowered rear bulkhead and strengthened sills and hinge pillars.

The revised 3.6 Coupe, announced on February 25, 1987, incorporated many changes, some – like the fully integrated ignition and 'micro-fuelling' injection – being externally invisible.

The 3.6 was finally given an automatic gearbox option in February 1987. This is the installation in the Cabriolet (note also the revised centre console).

Jaguar's own true Convertible appeared in the early spring of 1988, a graceful car that was an immediate success, especially in the USA. For several years, only the V12 engine was offered.

Almost as importantly, significant changes had been made to the power unit. Earlier on, the original 3.6-litre's undoubted raucousness at high rpm had been countered by revised timing chain tensioners, camshafts with a larger base circle diameter and reduced lift, and new steel bucket tappets in place of cast-iron ones. Now, on the back of the XJ40 programme, further refinements included replacing the previous electro-mechanical ignition system with a sophisticated fully electronic set-up which, combined with Bosch electronic fuel injection, gave an integrated engine management system. This 'microfuelling' arrangement gave better drivability, reliability and economy, the official urban cycle figure improving by 3.7mpg to 18.6mpg and the constant 75mph figure by 2.6mpg to 32mpg. Performance was stated to have remained unchanged, though torque had risen by 9lb ft to 249lb ft at 4,000rpm.

Many detail changes arrived at the same time. All XJ-S models now had heated door mirrors and washer jets, while heated seats with electrically operated lumbar support were optional on the 3.6 and standard on the V12, as were heated headlamp washers. A new centre console was finished in burr elm veneer on the 3.6 and burr walnut on the V12, and there

was redesigned console-mounted switchgear and a new steering wheel. Cruise control was now supplied by Hella, while the seat belt buckles were mounted on the seats rather than the floor.

Externally, Coupes were given a locking fuel filler cap (something the Cabriolets already had), and foglamps were fitted as standard to the V12 cars (and offered as extras on the six-cylinder models). All cars now had bright-finish stainless-steel door tread plates etched with the Jaguar name.

XJ-S 3.6 Sports Handling Pack
In September 1987, Jaguar made substantial chassis changes to the 3.6-litre XJ-S to differentiate more strongly between the six and 12-cylinder models. The 3.6 XJ-S was now firmly slanted towards the younger, more sporting driver. Front spring ratings went up by 43% and the rears by 3%, uprated Boge dampers were fitted all round, the front anti-roll bar diameter was increased and the rear anti-roll bar reintroduced in order to maintain balance.

Then, at last, the steering received the attention which many had felt it needed, the 3.6's power assistance being reduced and stiffer rack-mounting bushes specified. Wider-section Pirelli P600 235/60 VR tyres, optional at no extra cost,

With its Karmann-designed top erected, the Convertible XJ-S still looked attractive, while at speed it offered good refinement, too – not easy in a 150mph soft-top car!

Like the Cabriolet, the Convertible was a two-seater, although this time there was a single locker in the back.

completed the chassis changes, making the 3.6 a genuinely sporting car with a crisper turn-in and more controlled handling at the expense of only a moderately harsher ride. The marketplace liked the formula, and the 3.6 with its new Sports Handling Pack appealed to a wider range of customers.

Meanwhile, the writing was on the wall for the Cabriolet, and by September 1987 the six-cylinder version had gone, leaving the 5.3-litre version as the only open Jaguar for the time being – and then only until February 1988 when, concurrent with the adoption of Teves anti-lock braking on the XJ-S range, it too became obsolete.

So ended the production career of two most attractive Jaguars, which gained many admirers both during the time when they were current and in the years since. With the more recent Convertible being made in much greater numbers, they now have the further virtue of comparative rarity. Just 1,150 3.6-litre Cabriolets were made and 3,862 5.3-litre versions (of which 1,901 were sold in the USA), and good examples are now eagerly sought by enthusiasts.

The V12 Convertible

"A world-class, saleable XJ-S convertible on the Jaguar stand at the Geneva Show in March 1988!" That was the wording of John Egan's simple but challenging directive to the newly-formed project team – the first of its type at Jaguar – in May 1985. The 12-man team, drawn from all major functions within the factory, including engineering design, manufacturing, purchasing and marketing, was headed by Ken Giles and was the nearest thing to simultaneous engineering yet seen at Jaguar.

Having decided on the design concept, the team elected to employ Karmann of West Germany, with their great experience of building convertibles, to design the top, the special press tooling and the assembly jigs. Karmann also built the fully engineered prototypes (FEPs) on which the bulk of the engineering development programme was carried out. Much effort was put into arriving at the correct types and combinations of rubber mountings for the engine, front and rear subframes and suspension mountings for reduced shake and optimum refinement, some 30 combinations being evaluated at Jaguar's American test base in Phoenix, Arizona.

By March 1987, a year before the intended launch, prototypes were being completed from off-tool panels, and in November 1987, pre-production prototypes underwent final tests at MIRA and on local roads before being signed-off by the team and the Jaguar board.

The new model incorporated 108 new and 48 modified panels, about a third of the car's total panel count. The aim was to optimize refinement and to strengthen the shell around the transmission tunnel, the front and rear bulkheads and the rear floor area. Steel tubes were fitted within the sills and A-posts to further increase torsional rigidity.

The body was assembled at Jaguar's Castle Bromwich site, where AGVs (Automated Guided Vehicles) moved the bodies to different welding stations by following a wire buried in the floor – a new system which cost £3.6m to install.

Obviously, precision assembly of the hood frame was needed to ensure the best fit to the body, and the very strong frame was put together in the Browns Lane trim shop on a dedicated buck representing the car's cockpit. Tension straps and padding were then added before the high-quality fabric cover (available in black, blue and brown) was stretched over the frame. The completed hood met the car in the main assembly area and the hydraulic system was connected. Finally, the glass (heated) rear screen was added.

Electrically operated, the top, complete with its rear quarter windows, would lower in 12 seconds on pressing a single rocker switch on the centre console (after unlatching a lever

This is the XJ-S Collection Rouge, a 1989 special edition seen only in the USA; all were painted in signal red, the diamond-polished wheels were also picked out in red and there was a gold coachline.

on top of each A-post). The electric motor and hydraulic pump were carried in the luggage box behind the seats.

Dynamically, the new Convertible's performance was remarkably close to that of the Coupe's. At 1,900kg, it weighed 100kg more due to the body strengthening and hood-operating mechanism, yet top speed was put at 150mph, only 1mph less than the Coupe's – this thanks to the direct-glazed windscreen, effective window sealing and deletion of the front quarter-lights. Jaguar claimed that the convertible's 0–60mph time was only 0.3 second down on the closed car's. Suspension remained the traditional XJ-S V12 'soft' variety, partly because it was felt that stiffer suspension might invite scuttle shake in the open car. Wheels were new 6.5in x 15in 'lattice' alloys, adopted across the range.

Nor did the Convertible lack equipment: air conditioning remained standard, as did seat heating and electrically adjustable lumbar support. Burr walnut veneer featured on the facia and door cappings, where it was given intricate matchwood inlays, and on the centre console. Naturally, the braking system was the new Teves ABS introduced earlier in the year on all XJ-S models. The new Convertible was not cheap at its launch price of £36,000 in the UK, but it was certainly less expensive than the harsher-riding Mercedes SL range.

Jaguar had great hopes for the Convertible, especially in the US market. In particular, conquest sales from the dominant Mercedes SL convertible were hoped for – and indeed occurred; 2,014 V12 Convertibles were sold in the US in 1988, 2,556 in 1989, and a peak of 3,057 in 1990. By then it was accounting for about two-thirds of all XJ-S V12 sales worldwide, and during the first year of production, UK customers were having to join a 12-month waiting list – unless they paid up to £3,000 more than the by now £38,500 list price and bought from private speculators!

XJ-S Collection Rouge
Once again catering for their special market, Jaguar Cars Inc announced two unique North American models on June 16, 1989. However, the Vanden Plas Majestic sedan and the XJ-S Collection Rouge were UK-built and trimmed.

Standard mechanically, this special-edition XJ-S V12

Celebrating Jaguar's 1990 Le Mans win (the most recent in modern times), this XJ-S V12 Le Mans model was shown at the UK motor show that year; unmodified mechanically, it was distinguished by 'quad' headlights, special badging and many interior refinements.

For 1991, US customers could choose the XJ-S Classic Collection, with its gold-plated external badging and special interior.

featured Signal Red paintwork with a gold side-stripe, diamond-polished red-spoked wheels, unique rear badging, magnolia leather interior with bright red piping, magnolia leather-covered steering wheel and shift knob, and burred elm interior woodwork. The new variant cost $51,000 (against $48,000 for the normal Coupe and $57,000 for the Convertible) and was quite well received, even if its colour co-ordinates might not have been to British tastes!

The XJ-S for 1990

In December 1989, changes to the XJ-S for the 1990 model year took effect. The V12 engine continued with the new Marelli digital ignition system for enhanced smoothness, while a Sports Suspension Pack, similar in principle to that introduced on the 3.6 Coupe in 1987, was offered as a cost-option on XJ-S V12 Coupes. Minor interior changes included a new four-spoke, tilt-action steering wheel in place of the previous fore-and-aft adjustable type, redesigned stalk controls, and an ignition switch moved from the facia to the steering column. In the US, the XJ-S Collection Rouge adopted this new specification, too. December 1989 was also notable, of course, for the confirmation of Ford's takeover of Jaguar Cars for £1.6 billion – a development that was soon to have a huge impact on Jaguar's design and manufacturing philosophy.

Changes to the XJ-S during 1990 were few, though a sign of the times was the adoption of catalytic converters for the V12 as standard in virtually all markets (the exception being a few Far Eastern states where unleaded petrol was not available).

One new XJ-S variant did appear, though, at the UK's International Motor Show at the NEC, Birmingham, in September 1990, alongside the just-announced 3.2-litre XJ6 saloon range. The Le Mans Special Edition XJ-S V12, unlike the 1988 Le Mans commemorative model (*see Chapter 7*), was not a JaguarSport offering, but a unique Jaguar model based on a mechanically standard 5.3-litre XJ-S Coupe.

The 280 cars built featured 'quad' headlights (similar to the US-specification XJ-S), 16in forged alloy lattice wheels, sports suspension, a full Autolux leather interior with new seating, high-contrast walnut veneer on the facia and door cappings, a four-spoke leather steering wheel and Wilton carpeting. The stainless-steel sill plates displayed a Le Mans V12 motif and the limited-edition serial number.

North America did not receive the 'Le Mans' but instead marketed their own special-edition XJ-S in the form of the Classic Collection. Announced in October 1990, both Coupe and Convertible V12 models were given unique paint and trim combinations, the latter in light colours – magnolia and doeskin with contrasting piping. The matching leather gearshift knob and warm charcoal-toned leather steering wheel were also special. Gold-plated badges on trunk and bonnet denoted the (mechanically standard) cars' status.

In November, Venture Pressings opened for business; jointly owned by Jaguar and GKN, it would soon be producing all XJ-S body panels, taking over from Rover's Swindon press shop. Greater control and thus greater quality was Jaguar's aim, a prelude to the final and most far-reaching changes Jaguar were to make to the XJ-S.

The 1996-model XJS was named the Celebration; this is the 4.0 Convertible.

50

CHAPTER 6

Four litres and a facelift

But the flying buttresses remain

Despite an apparent lack of activity on the XJ-S front during 1990, Jaguar's engineers – including the same project team which had successfully evolved the Convertible – had been very busy with what amounted to a fundamental redesign of the car. All was revealed on May 1, 1991.

Visually, this was the most ambitious upgrade of the car since its 1975 launch. Most obvious was the restyled rear end, which now featured a broad chrome embellishment across the trunk lid and new rectangular, neutral-density lights. Then there was an extended glass area for the rear side windows, and gone were the front quarter-lights. The nose of the car changed least, the grille simply reverting to black underneath a new plated embellisher which ran along the bonnet's leading edge. The sills were now flared front and rear.

Changes continued throughout the car. Inside, after 15 years the idiosyncratic barrel-type minor instruments finally vanished in favour of a new instrument pack with traditional, crisp, white-on-black analogue dials set into a burr walnut (instead of elm) veneer panel. New sports front seats and redesigned rear seats were other major interior changes.

Another overdue upgrade was the replacement of the 3.6-litre engine with the 4.0-litre AJ6 unit, which had made its bow in the XJ6 saloon back in September 1989; power output thus rose from 199 to 223bhp (both 'catalyst' figures), which was worth around half a second off the 0–60mph time and added some 4mph to the maximum speed. The 4.0-litre unit came with either the uprated ZF 4HP24 automatic gearbox (which had a 30% higher torque-handling capacity) or the Getrag 290, three-plane-gate, manual five-speed gearbox –

this latter a considerable improvement on the clumsier five-plane 265 box used on the XJ-S 3.6. The XJ6 4.0-litre's twin-mass flywheel arrived with this box, too.

Suspension remained the 'sports' type for the six-cylinder car, the V12 sticking with the original softer settings (although sports suspension had become an option on the V12 Coupe).

The most fundamental change of all, though, concerned the bodyshell. Of the car's 490 panels, 180 were replaced or modified – enough to have made quite drastic changes to the car's outward appearance, but, argued chief stylist Geoff Lawson, the car's basic shape was now a 'classic', and neither he nor Jaguar wished to interrupt the continually improving clinic response to the XJ-S by risking changes. In other words, the Coupe's flying buttresses were to remain!

The real benefits of the revised bodyshell lay, however, in better fit and finish, durability and more economic production. The new XJS (the hyphen was intentionally dropped to emphasize the facelift) was the first car to use panels from Venture Pressings, as already noted, the Telford-based press shop which had been set up jointly by Jaguar and GKN-Sankey. The bodies were assembled at Castle Bromwich where almost £4m was spent on a modern computer-controlled welding process, while new quality disciplines learnt from Ford contributed much to the success of the re-engineered car.

For increased corrosion-resistance, all critical body panels were now zinc-coated, there was zinc phosphate pre-treatment, cathodic electrocoating and wax-injected box-sections. A clear-over-base paint system was used, with two base colours and two clear coats.

Although it had many new body panels the new 4.0-litre retained the basic XJS shape, especially at the front; the bonnet gained a bright finisher and light units were new (the US model was given similar units in place of the previous quad lamps).

Rear end changes were more radical, with new rectangular lights and bright trunk-lid finisher. Side window glass was extended to replace the extractor vents (resited on the 'B' post shut face), but cabin light area was actually unchanged. The lower edge of the bonded rear screen was brought back adjacent to the trunk aperture, increasing rake and glass area. Note the new fuel filler flap.

Badging on all models was restyled and transferred from the vertical trunk panel to the upper section. There was no longer a dash between XJ and S, either!

The 4.0-litre engine, first seen in the XJ6 in the autumn of 1989, owed its increased capacity to a longer stroke. The scuttle air intake panel in the foreground changed from black to body colour.

With the 4.0-litre came a choice of facia colours to augment the upholstery colour. The lighting switch was transferred from the dash to the left-hand stalk and electric seat-adjustment controls (now standard) were on the door casing.

Naturally, the V12 XJS was upgraded in the same way, while its 5.3-litre engine was given a completely new Lucas 26 CU fuel control system for easier starting and better warm-up running. It also gave the on-board diagnosis facility which had become mandatory in smog-conscious California. Additionally, the fuel rail and injectors were revised and the underbonnet layout tidied – most of the pipework vanished and there was a new inlet manifold casting bearing the inscription 'Jaguar V12'.

These changes helped raise maximum power from 273 to 280bhp, regaining some of the lost efficiency incurred by the catalyst exhaust and bringing the 0–60mph time comfortably under 8 seconds once again.

The new range brought price rises, but they were moderate: the cheapest XJS, the manual 4.0-litre Coupe, was now £33,400 and the V12 Convertible £43,500 – but looking extremely good value compared with such as the BMW 850i at £61,950.

Initially, the revised range did not include a 4.0-litre Convertible; that came a year later, in May 1992, when it incorporated all the relevant updates, but was available only with automatic transmission. A pioneering feature was an optional driver's-side airbag, the first offered on a Jaguar; available on all the XJS range, it added £700 to the price.

At the same time came a new, stainless-steel tubular underbody bracing member on both the 4.0 and 5.3-litre Convertibles; the rear legs of this X-frame mounted on the jacking points under the footwells, the front legs on the front crossmember beneath the radiator (these attachment points had been built into the shell at the 1991 facelift). The frame acted in tension to increase the body's resistance to twisting and provided an extra 25% torsional rigidity, markedly reducing shudder.

The 4.0 Convertible – still with just two seats – was available at first in the UK and Europe only, and did not arrive in the US until later (the revised XJS V12 had been sold there since July 1991).

New for 1993

In September 1992, the 1993 model year Jaguars were

Finally gone were the unconventional barrel-type minor instruments; it is surprisingly expensive to re-engineer an instrument panel, which is why the change wasn't made earlier.

The Getrag 290 three-plane manual gearbox replaced the more awkward five-plane 265; note the cruise control switch on the console.

announced; while this time the saloons received most attention, there were improvements to the XJS as well. Manual transmission now became an option on the 4.0-litre Convertible, while for those who wanted the maximum comfort, the Convertible's 'soft' suspension became an option on the 4.0-litre Coupe (for which the sports suspension remained the standard specification). To even further improve rigidity, rear underfloor struts were added to both the 5.3 and 4.0 Convertibles.

All cars had a redesigned steering column to provide a more comfortable driving position, the wheel now being 2 inches further away from the driver. Battery and alternator capacities were increased, too. The seat slides were given more rearward travel, new velour cloth upholstery replaced the tweed cloth, and the automatic cars received a new T-shaped selector lever. There was an evaporative loss emissions control system, and a driver's-side airbag was standardized across the full XJS range.

After British Government tax changes, the most expensive XJS was now the V12 Convertible at £48,864, and the most

New box pleating featured on the restyled front sports seats; the rear of the interior was also restyled with new rear-quarter and parcel shelf trim. The centre-section housed the seat buckles, and the 'B' post shoulder anchorage for front seat belts was now adjustable.

The V12 Convertible in its new guise, with check wheels. The open cars remained as two-seaters.

Interior of a May 1991 V12 Convertible, naturally featuring the new instrument panel.

Framing the much-revised XJS body at Castle Bromwich; the front inner wings and roof panel are being spot-welded here.

An XJS Coupe receiving its doors at Castle Bromwich; the bolt-on front wings would be added next. The panel-fit and longevity of the XJS body were much improved from May 1991 onwards.

The revised 4.0-litre Convertible arrived a year after the V12 version, in May 1992.

The XJS was the first Jaguar to be offered with an airbag, initially available as an option and on the driver's side only.

affordable was the 4.0-litre manual-transmission Coupe at £32,544.

In the US market, the XJS model range for 1993 was reduced to just two models, the 4.0-litre Coupe ($49,750) and the 4.0-litre Convertible ($56,750), both in 223bhp 'emissions' configuration with automatic gearbox. Due largely to the 'gas guzzler' tax, temporarily no XJS V12s were being sold in the US. However, the XJS 4.0-litre Convertible proved highly popular there, and in 1993 sold 1,866 units, or three times the 4.0-litre Coupe total!

Not that American customers were denied the V12 entirely, because at the Detroit Auto Show in January there was displayed a US edition of the XJR-S 6.0-litre; just 100 – 50 Coupes and (uniquely) 50 Convertibles – were scheduled to be sold in North America during 1993. They were priced at $73,000 and $80,100 respectively. Additionally, from February 1993 it became possible to order an XJS 4.0 with a five-speed manual gearbox – and/or the sports suspension could also be ordered on the Coupe for the first time in the US.

They may have looked insubstantial but, acting in torsion, the new underfloor bracing tubes fitted from May 1992 markedly reduced body shudder in the open cars.

The 1993-model XJS V12 Coupe; outwardly the closed car was little changed.

The ultimate luxury XJS of its day was the low-volume Insignia, available to special order from October 1992 and personalized by such as White Pearl paintwork (£1,900 extra), special leather interior (£3,000) and various wheel finishes (£350). These touches were added by Jaguar's SVO department, staffed mainly by craftsmen who had formerly built the Daimler DS 420 Limousine.

The 6.0-litre Convertible with the '93½' model year bumper fairings; the front spoiler now incorporated brake cooling slots. Note the alloy wheels.

Six litres, four seats and colour-keying

The next major change for the XJS came in May 1993, when the '1993½' model year cars were announced. These incorporated a whole package of improvements 'to strengthen the appeal and competitiveness' of the cars. The big news was an increase in capacity to 6.0 litres for the V12 which was now mated to a new four-speed automatic gearbox. The Convertibles received 2-plus-2 seating (though a two-seater version was available to special order), and moulded, colour-keyed bumpers front and rear (similar to those used on the now-defunct XJR-S) were adopted as standard XJS wear. Along with new suspension settings came outboard rear brakes – the first big change to Jaguar's independent rear suspension since it appeared on the E-type and Mk 10 in 1961. The chief aim was to improve handbrake performance, though getting heat away from the final-drive unit must have been worthwhile. New calipers were also specified.

Launched earlier that year in the new XJ12 and Daimler Double Six saloons, the latest V12 engine's increased capacity of 5,994cc had been achieved by lengthening the stroke from 70mm to 78.5mm. Cylinder head, inlet valves, camshaft profile (for improved refinement), flat-top pistons and a forged instead of cast-iron crankshaft were all new, there was also a new low-loss catalyst exhaust system, and despite a lower compression ratio (now 11:1), power was up by 10% to 308bhp at 5,350rpm and peak torque by 16% to 355lb ft at 2,850rpm, restoring performance eroded by emission equipment.

Jaguar claimed that the Coupe's top speed had gone up from 147mph to 161mph, rather more than would be expected from the modest horsepower increase, so gearing probably had as much to do with it. Likewise, the 0–60mph time was over a second better at 6.6 seconds.

The lively feel of the car from rest was enhanced by a new torque converter (with lock-up clutch), which improved take-

Extra cubic capacity helped replace horsepower lost by the ever more restrictive emission regulations. Notice how much tidier the V12 engine bay had become by this time (May 1993).

The first major change to the Heynes/Knight independent rear suspension also came in 1993, when the rear brakes were taken outboard. This photograph shows XJS rear suspension assemblies being built up at Browns Lane in mid-1995.

It had taken almost five years, but at last owners of the Convertible had the benefit of rear seats.

The hydraulic pump for the power top was relocated above the battery alongside the spare wheel on the 2-plus-2 Convertibles.

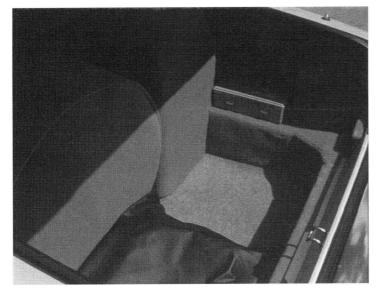

off, while at last the V12 XJS was given four ratios, thanks to the GM4L80-E transmission now being fitted. In fact this used the same geartrain as before, but an extra, fourth, overdrive ratio was provided, allowing the final-drive ratio to be dropped to 3.54:1. This got rid of the previous 'overtaking gap' between 40 and 50mph.

Sport and Normal modes featured with this box; with the latter selected, starts were made in second, whereas in Sport, the car started in first and more readily made part-throttle kickdowns. Shift quality was improved as the new gearbox was able to communicate electronically with the new Lucas Marelli engine management system to trigger a reduction in engine torque during shifts.

Both the 4.0 and 6.0-litre Coupes were given newly-developed sports suspension as standard: spring and front anti-roll bar rates were actually reduced, but extra precision was provided by Bilstein dampers and the deletion of the rear anti-roll bar. Front suspension castor was increased from 3.5 to 5 degrees to improve straight-line running. With this set-up came low-profile Pirelli P600 225/55 ZR16 sport tyres which,

The gear selector on automatic cars now featured a 'T' handle; this is a V12 car, which now also enjoyed four speeds.

Sun visors incorporated an illuminated vanity mirror from May 1993.

of course, put back some stiffness; they came on new 16in x 7in cast-alloy spoked wheels – these being common to all variants, though the previous 16in forged lattice alloy wheel continued as a cost-option.

Both Convertibles remained on unaltered, Boge-damped 'touring' suspension, with Pirelli's 'comfort' P4000E 225/60 ZR16 tyres, but for the first time, thanks to the stiffened bodyshells, purchasers of Convertibles could specify the sports suspension and P600 tyres. A no-cost option on all models was a space-saver alloy spare wheel, measuring 3½in x 18in, with a 115/85 R18 tyre. Finally, a ZF steering rack now replaced the Adwest item, mainly for better quality and reliability.

The new 2-plus-2 Convertible had arrived only after some prevarication from sales departments, particularly in the United States, where at first the concept was met with disinterest, and the project began in a low-key manner within

Jaguar's Special Vehicle Operations. Then America became keen and the project went mainstream, with Motor Panels (a company once owned by Jaguar) carrying out the prototype programme and later supplying unique body panels. The rear seating meant virtually creating a new body in white, with a new sub-assembly welded on top of the existing underframe to form a rear seat pan and back in place of the rear stowage boxes of the two-seater. As an added bonus, this stiffened the shell considerably at this point.

To make room for the rear seats, the hydraulic pump for the top was relocated on top of the battery in the boot, while the rear screen was now slightly shallower to enable it and the top to be folded behind the rear seats without increasing the stack height. Hood material changed from cloth to Ambla, colour-keyed to the interior.

Inside, further changes included sun-visors with built-in

The curvaceous new bumper mouldings complemented the XJS's shape well; note the placement of repeater and fog warning lights, and the elliptical exhaust pipes – last seen on the SS Jaguar 100 and its contemporaries!

vanity mirrors and lights (an essential for the US market!), improved air conditioning with a cold-air intake, ambient-air sensor and motorized aspirator, and warning chimes which sounded for 6 seconds if the driver's seat was occupied but the seat belt was not being worn. A new alarm system was standard on all XJS models.

The exterior changes certainly modernized the car, and if you wondered why the colour-keyed bumper mouldings were not brought in with the new rear-end styling in May 1991, the reason was lack of resources: Jaguar's styling department under Geoff Lawson had in fact evolved all these new exterior features as a single package back in, believe it or not, 1985...

Pricing remained highly competitive, especially in view of the many improvements. The 4.0-litre XJS Coupe was the most reasonably priced at £33,600, while the flagship V12 2-plus-2 Convertible, at £52,900, became the most expensive model in Jaguar's line-up, being £1,200 more than the Daimler Double Six saloon.

The revised 4.0-litre Coupe went on sale in the US on July 1, 1993, followed by the 2-plus-2 Convertible and the 6.0-litre range on August 1.

The XJS for 1994
Not content with the large-scale changes brought in during 1993, in September of that year Jaguar announced further improvements for the 1994 model year. There was a new air conditioning control panel featuring a driver-controlled demist with separate switch, a recirculation switch which isolated the cockpit from traffic fumes, and an on/off control for the refrigeration compressor. Also, a non-CFC refrigerant was now used. All cars were given a new rear-view interior mirror, and on the Convertible, a burgundy option brought the total

The 1994-model 4.0 Coupe was offered with optional five-speed transmission in the US, the first time the XJS had been catalogued there with a manual gearbox. Sports suspension was also on offer.

June 1994 saw the appearance of the AJ16-engined XJS; this is the 4.0 Coupe, with the new colour-keyed grille, headlight surrounds and door mirrors.

The AJ16 was almost a new engine;
under the new cam cover (in denser
magnesium for extra refinement)
lay new camshafts, and there was
sequential fuel injection and a new
throttle system.

Coupe rear seats were now styled
as for the 2-plus-2; standard upholstery for the 4.0-litre was cloth, but
this car has the optional leather.

New audio equipment featured with a radio having RDS-EON for local traffic information; the faceplate was detachable for security reasons.

What with passenger airbags now appearing, stowage space was even tighter in the XJS, so elasticated map pockets on the front seats were welcome additions.

hood colour choice up to five. On the safety front, a passenger airbag was now standard, taking the place of the glovebox behind a veneered deployment lid.

The 4.0-litre engine was given a new camshaft cover with integral oil filler (doing away with the separate filler tube), an integral crankcase breather system and a 13-bolt fixing for improved oil sealing. There was also a new one-piece cast inlet manifold with integral rampipes.

Then, to avoid inadvertent use of the accelerator pedal as 'Drive' was engaged, all automatic-transmission cars were given an interlock system whereby the gearshift selector could only be moved from 'Park' if the ignition was switched on and the footbrake applied. A new vehicle security system was also offered, using an electronic pass key with random code generation.

AJ16 adds refinement

A revised six-cylinder engine was introduced during the early summer of 1994. The changes were substantial enough in scale to warrant a new designation – AJ16 – and power output was up 7% to 244bhp (237bhp for US-spec engines) at 4,700rpm; but the need to meet future emissions regulations and to increase refinement for the new X300 saloon due that September were the major reasons for the upgrade.

Incorporated within AJ16's new block and head were improved induction porting, new cam profiles, a higher compression, new pistons and a new Generic Engine Management System (GEMS) to comply with forthcoming US legislation requiring further on-board diagnosis capability (OBD II, whereby the engine's systems can detect and report faults). This came with sequential fuel injection timing, a new throttle system and a low-loss catalyst exhaust system. In the drive-train, the 4.0-litre automatic now had a low-inertia torque converter to improve off-the-line performance and provide smoother changes.

Both 4.0 and 6.0 models were given redesigned trim with the Coupe's rear seats now of similar appearance to the 2-plus-2 Convertible's; the V12 was all-leather inside, with restyled front seats having ruche centre panels and contrasting piping. The 4.0 had what was termed sculptured cloth seats as standard, leather being a cost option.

Externally there were further moves to differentiate between models, the sporting nature of the 4.0-litre being emphasized by additional colour-keying (grille, headlight surrounds and door mirrors). The V12 retained a black grille and chrome bumper cappings, with new and discreet V12 badging on the front wings complementing painted twin coachlines. Wheels

were five-spoke alloy on the 4.0-litre, 20-spoke diamond-turned alloy on the 6.0-litre; chrome-plated five-spoke alloys were a cost-option on either car.

Despite a quoted 0–60mph acceleration time of 6.9 seconds and a top speed of 147mph, the 4.0 contrived to be more economical on fuel, with an official 37.2mpg at a constant 50mph. The AJ16's level of refinement was now such that it rivalled the V12's... In the US, the 4.0-litre had posted a 45% sales increase by the end of 1994, nearly 4,300 finding delighted new owners, and worldwide XJS sales were up 21% on the 1993 figure.

The XJS Celebration models
During 1995 Jaguar achieved its 60th year and the XJS was the model selected to highlight the anniversary in the product range. Announced in May 1995, the Celebration cars were

This Federal XJS Coupe was displayed at the April 1995 New York Show and, finished in bright red, it more than held its own against products 20 years younger.

An XJS Celebration Convertible showing the wood-rim wheel, integral head restraints and generally upgraded interior.

little changed mechanically, except that the XJ6's new vacuum-assisted brakes were fitted; these were claimed to provide improvements in pedal effort and sensitivity, particularly when check-braking, while also requiring less driver effort to hold the car against the torque converter when stationary in traffic.

The Celebration model was given a more luxurious interior with 4.0-litre cars being brought more or less in line with the V12. Both the Coupe and the Convertible had leather seat facings, with integral head restraints embossed with the leaping jaguar. The central console lid was also leather-trimmed, while the veneer was now figured sapwood walnut. Wood was also featured on the gearshift knob and the new steering wheel.

Externally, the most noticeable change were the Aerosport 7 x 16in cast-alloy wheels carrying a new centre badge featuring the 'growler' on a black background (five-spoked chrome alloy wheels remained an option). Radiator grilles were now finished in black, door mirrors and rear number-plate surround were chrome-plated, and there was a distinctive enamelled bonnet badge with a gold jaguar growler on a green background (no Celebration badge as such, however). There was a choice of 17 exterior colours plus five for the Convertible's top.

These changes came with modest price rises for the 4.0-litre; in the UK the automatic Coupe was now £38,950 as opposed to £38,250 and the Convertible £45,950. However, the already quite pricey V12 was unchanged from 1994 at £50,500 for the Coupe and £58,800 for the Convertible.

It was the 4.0-litre that Jaguar promoted at the Celebration's launch; V12 sales had dwindled, including in the US, perhaps because the price differential was no longer so justified over the consistently upgraded 4.0, which now gave so little away in either refinement or, for most practical purposes,

Available to special order only after the summer of 1995, this is one of the last XJS V12 Coupes, equipped with Aerosport alloy wheels. The very last V12, a red Coupe, is being retained by the Jaguar Daimler Heritage Trust.

The AJ16 4.0-litre engine was destined to be the power unit which would see the XJS into triumphant obsolescence.

71

Twenty years on from the model's launch, all the major XJS variants are on parade with (clockwise from left) a 3.6 Cabriolet, a 1976 5.3 Coupe, a 5.3 HE Coupe, a Celebration 6.0 Coupe and a 4.0 Celebration Convertible.

performance to the larger-engined car. Series production of the V12 tailed off during the summer of 1995 and by the autumn it was obtainable only to special order.

So the 4.0-litre was destined to see out the XJS in 1996, when after an astonishing 21 years the old would finally make way for the new. In fact, from the latter part of 1995 through to the first half of 1996, customers were being offered a guaranteed 80% return (given modest condition and mileage qualifications) if they bought a new XJS and traded it in when the replacement car appeared.

Codenamed X100, and with a floorpan loosely based on the XJS's, the otherwise all-new sporting Jaguar would take over – and add to – the XJS's role before the year was out. But while a more overtly sporting car, and representing a quantum leap forward dynamically, the XK8 is very unlikely to match the sheer staying power of the enigmatic XJS, a car that had achieved so much more in both acceptability and sheer enjoyment of ownership than the most optimistic of forecasters would have ventured to predict way back in 1975 when it was launched.

CHAPTER 7

Modified and JaguarSport cars

Scalding the cat: performance and bodywork conversions

Note: The companies included here are those particularly aligned to the XJ-S or who have offered significantly different coachwork options; their addresses will be found in Appendix G, along with those of companies offering more general services to the XJ-S owner.

JaguarSport

Although way back in 1977 Group 44, in North America, had successfully taken the XJ-S racing and TWR had done the same in Europe from 1982 – both teams with manufacturer backing – it was not until August 1988 that an official 'performance' version of the car appeared. This was the V12-engined XJR-S Coupe, the first offering from the newly-formed JaguarSport Ltd.

JaguarSport, owned 50/50 by Jaguar and Tom Walkinshaw's TWR Group, was formed in May 1988 and charged with the objective of producing visually and dynamically different sporting variants based on current production models. These would trade on the reputation established not only by the TWR XJ-S, but also by the TWR Jaguar Group C XJR series of sports-racing cars, by then coming good and winners of the 1988 Le Mans 24 Hours race.

JaguarSport began operating at Kidlington, the home of the (entirely separate) TWR Jaguar race team, and it was hoped that, without cutting corners on quality or durability, the smaller organization would be able to reduce lead times and create new sub-models rather more quickly than Jaguar's Whitley engineering centre (which in any case was busy with new mainstream projects).

In this they were certainly successful, and the cars which evolved – both XJ-S and XJ40-derived – effectively extended Jaguar's model range and market at a time when major new-model action was not possible. The cars themselves, developed with considerable input from Tom Walkinshaw himself, looked and felt sporting and gave exemplary handling without destroying the smooth-rolling Jaguar 'feel' – something of which so many non-factory conversions have been guilty. Although sales might not have achieved initial expectations – few foresaw the slump of the early 1990s – between 1988 and 1993 the JaguarSport operation produced probably 50 times as many altered cars than all the private specialists put together.

To obtain a JaguarSport model, UK customers initially were required to place their orders with one of 20 selected Jaguar dealers (later the arrangement was widened to include all Jaguar dealers). Cars were built at Browns Lane to a JaguarSport 'add and delete' list, arriving at Kidlington minus bumpers, but already trimmed to JaguarSport specification. The special JaguarSport adornments were then added and the car taken back to Jaguar for despatch to the dealer.

The original 1988 XJR-S was based on the modified, factory-approved TWR XJ-S V12 Coupe which TWR had offered privately since 1984 – specifically the body equipment and some suspension parts, not the more exotic 6.0-litre and manual gearbox conversions (TWR ceased to market their own Jaguar modifications on the formation of JaguarSport, incidentally). The JaguarSport XJ-S Coupe was thus endowed with a colour-keyed, glassfibre front airdam, side skirts, rear apron and boot-mounted wing. Although the 5.3-litre, 291bhp

The TWR Group had developed a range of Jaguar-approved performance components for the XJ-S during the mid-1980s; this is a TWR JaguarSport Coupe fitted with Speedline wheels and body kit and photographed in 1986. TWR also offered a manual gearbox conversion for the V12, but found the take-up was not high and so it did not become a JaguarSport option.

engine remained standard, suspension changes featured 11% stiffer front springs, specially valved Bilstein dampers all round, rear radius arm front bushes 20% less compliant, stiffer steering rack mountings and a revalved power steering pinion, giving less assistance. Wheels were Speedline alloys with 7.5in rims and wider, lower-profile Pirelli P600 235/60 VR-15 tyres.

While outright performance was not enhanced, these modifications made a great difference to the way the XJ-S felt and, because of the greater cornering power and reduced roll, made it a quicker and more satisfying car to drive over demanding roads.

The first 100 examples – all sold, it was claimed, within four days of announcement – were nominated Le Mans Celebration models to mark Jaguar's historic 1988 victory. Each of these cars had special, individually numbered sill plates and were painted Tungsten Grey with grey-piped doeskin upholstery. They cost the same as the normal XJR-S: £35,000, or £3,000 more than the standard XJ-S V12 Coupe.

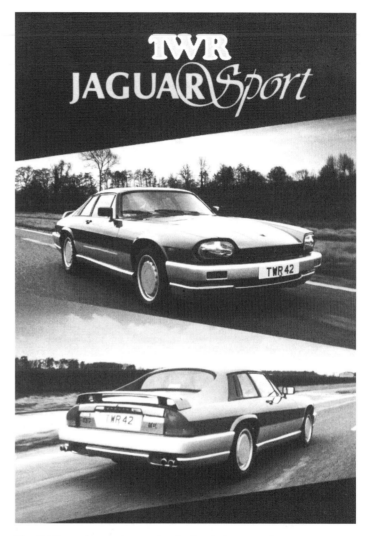

The TWR catalogue shows clearly the derivation of the JaguarSport name; while the 'official' car adopted the same body fairings, these were not normally finished in the contrasting tone seen on the TWR version shown here. (*Illustration: Ian Cooling Collection*)

The XJR-S was launched in August 1988 "as a tribute to the Le Mans-winning XJR-9". Initially available in the UK only, it was priced at £38,500.

XJR-S badging featured on the rear end along with a trunklid-mounted spoiler (this having a strategically-placed hole for the aerial). Paint colours were Signal Red, Regency Red, Black, Solent Blue, Silver Frost and Brooklands Green (plus Tungsten Grey for the 1988 Celebration model).

The car was praised for its increased agility, but the absence of extra power disappointed some testers. *Autocar*, indeed, found their test car's poor 0–60mph time of 9.3 seconds hard to believe – some 2sec slower than earlier standard automatic-transmission road-test cars. However, it so happened that at about this time (mid-1989) Jaguar had dropped the V12's compression ratio from 12.6 to 11.5:1 so that it could use lower octane unleaded fuel, thereby reducing power from 291 to some 285bhp and inevitably affecting straight-line performance.

Some 300 of the first XJR-S Coupes were sold when, after almost exactly a year, a considerably more ambitious version was announced. The new XJR-S used a JaguarSport-developed and built 6.0-litre engine, its extra 648cc obtained from a special long-stroke crankshaft (78.5mm instead of 70mm). Aided by Zytek sequential injection, a digital ignition system and modified cold air intakes, power was lifted from 291bhp at 5,500rpm to 318bhp at 5,250rpm.

Another look was taken at the chassis, too: the wheel rim width went up by 0.5in to 8in and the diameter from 15in to

Inside the XJR-S the leather-covered steering wheel and shift knob (instead of a 'T' handle) were colour-keyed to the interior. Standard XJ-S sports seats were fitted, but they usually came with contrasting piping and stitching.

The first 100 XJR-S Coupes celebrated Jaguar's 1988 Le Mans victory and stainless-steel sill plates carried each car's unique number. Purchasers were also given a day's high-speed driving tuition at Silverstone, plus a ride with a TWR Jaguar team driver in an XJR-9.

16in to allow new lower-profile tyres to be fitted, unusually of different sections front and rear – 225/50 front and 245/55 rear, both Dunlop D40 M22. Front spring rates were increased significantly (but, interestingly, were still not as stiff as those of Jaguar's own Sports pack) and the previously standard rear springs were replaced by stiffer ones.

These measures made the car even more taut, but Tom Walkinshaw was at pains to ensure that the basic comfort levels customers expected of a Jaguar were retained. The least sporting aspect of the car remained the GM 400 three-speed automatic gearbox, which continued to blunt its cross-country progress a little. But straight-line performance was restored, *Autocar & Motor* (the two rival British weeklies had now merged) crediting their road test XJR-S 6.0-litre with a 0–60mph time of 7.1 seconds, with 100mph coming up in 17.7 seconds. (Nevertheless, a perfectly standard HE automatic, also with a 2.88:1 final-drive and weighing about the same, had given 6.5 seconds and 16.7 seconds when tested by *Autocar* back in April 1982…meeting emission standards had certainly exacted a penalty.)

The XJR-S finally received a power boost when the 6.0-litre appeared in the autumn of 1989. Externally the car was little altered, but the new engine clawed back some of the performance lost by emissions controls. Four exhaust outlets helped identify the XJR-S 6.0-litre, while suspension had been further refined; tyres were now Goodyear Eagles, a change stemming from the TWR Jaguar race team's association with the American tyre company.

The XJR-S V12 boasted red camshaft covers with the familiar JaguarSport logo. The 6.0-litre engine gave 318bhp, indisputably more than any previous XJ-S.

On all-round ability the XJR-S still shone when compared with its rivals. In 1991 the respected British monthly *Performance Car* matched a 6.0-litre XJR-S (£45,500) against an Aston Martin Virage (£129,950), BMW 850i (£59,500), Mercedes 500SL (£63,460) and Porsche 928S4 (£64,496) over a two-day, 1,000-mile excursion from London to Scotland, and for most testers the veteran became first choice: 'The Jaguar XJR-S is a special car, possessing a smooth-riding yet fabulously responsive chassis with communicative steering and tireless brakes. And what an engine. Lusty enough to make three gears seem plenty, silent at a cruise, subtly rorty but still silky smooth when worked hard, the 6.0-litre V12 is perfectly matched to the role of Grand Touring. The XJR-S isn't perfect by any means – it's dated and thirsty – but when it comes to delivering satisfaction on the long haul, it is without peers...'

It was at the Frankfurt Motor Show on September 11, 1991 that a 'new' XJR-S was announced. The latest model, available from January 1992 in the UK and Europe, used the 'facelift' XJS which had appeared in May 1991 as its basis. It

A 1990-model XJR-S 6.0-litre interior, showing contrasting piping to the seats. Sill plates carried the JaguarSport motif, and the seat headrests were embossed with the XJR initials.

thus took advantage of the latter's re-engineered bodyshell and many detail improvements. New, more subtle and better-integrated body styling add-ons featured, this time from Geoff Lawson's styling department at Whitley, and the special 6.0-litre engine gained more power.

A less restrictive catalyst exhaust system was responsible for most of this, along with revised engine management; 338bhp at 5,250rpm was now quoted, up some 15bhp, and torque was slightly increased, too. JaguarSport claimed a 0–60mph time of 6.5 seconds – still only equalling the previous best road-test result, but the latest XJR-S did have a catalyst exhaust system (not to mention the three-speed, power-absorbing GM 400 automatic transmission).

Suspension modifications remained much the same except that the Bilsteins were revalved to suit the new tyres fitted – Goodyear Eagle ZR replacing Dunlop D40 M22. Writing about the car in *Jaguar World*, early in 1992, I expressed the view that the XJR-S was now probably the best all-round Jaguar built, not excepting the mainstream XJS V12, even when equipped with the now-optional Sports pack, which some considered gave a less satisfactory low-speed ride.

Quality was improving all the time, and with the 1992 model-year XJ-S 6.0-litre, the entire JaguarSport procedure – both parts and processes – had to go through the same full factory approval and validation procedure that mainstream models underwent.

Early on, owners could fit JaguarSport equipment as after-market kits available through Jaguar dealers, including the body styling parts applicable to their model-year car. The XJ-S suspension kit cost £1,157, for instance, in 1990. When JaguarSport moved to new Oxfordshire premises at Wykham Mill, Bloxham (where the XJ220 and, much later, the XJS-based Aston Martin DB7 were also assembled) this initiative was developed into the 'FAB' scheme whereby a standard XJ-S or XJ6 could be 'Fitted At Bloxham' with all the parts necessary to turn it into the JaguarSport version (except the JaguarSport badge itself, which was reserved for JaguarSport cars sold new).

Again, all this was done via the local dealer who arranged for the vehicle to be taken to Bloxham for the work; the scheme gave the owner the satisfaction of knowing that the conversion was carried out to 'factory' standards by JaguarSport itself.

There was no official JaguarSport XJS 4.0-litre, and the XJR-S faded from the scene when the standard V12 XJS also went to 6.0 litres in May 1993. The latter's production 6.0-litre engine was developed by Jaguar and built at the Radford engine plant, unlike the slightly more powerful and much more expensive JaguarSport version, each example of which had taken two men five days to build. The new car also had the great advantage of, at last, a four-speed automatic transmission. No official JaguarSport four-speed XJR-S was built, it appears, but owners of the new standard 6.0-litre could and sometimes did have their cars 'Fitted At Bloxham' with the XJR-S body, suspension and steering kits, thereby gaining the best of both worlds.

Most JaguarSport items for the XJ-S continue to be available from Jaguar dealers at the time of writing (1996), while because of the comparatively small numbers made, and its effective, well-coordinated and durable specification, the XJR-S is already arousing interest amongst enthusiasts.

Arden Automobilau GmbH

Undoubtedly the most prolific producer of modified Jaguars on the Continent, Arden, with the demise of JaguarSport Ltd,

The final XJR-S model picked up the new rear-end styling of the latest XJS (launched the previous May), with its horizontal lights and chrome embellishments.

The 1992-model JaguarSport 6.0-litre V12 gave more power, thanks to more sophisticated engine management and an exhaust system that was actually less restrictive than the previous non-catalyst one.

is also unique in now being the only private company marketing Jaguar-approved performance parts and conversions. Founded by Jochen Arden, who at the time of writing is still only in his forties, Arden Automobilau is also unique as being the smallest company accepted by the German government as an actual car manufacturer – so radical are some of Arden's reworkings.

Many variations on the XJ-S have been offered at various times by Arden, including their own convertible (pre-dating Jaguar's by three years), a remodelled Coupe with the flying buttresses deleted, 'plus two' conversions for the two-seater XJ-S Cabriolets and Convertibles (70 of these were completed in 1991 alone, some with Arden-designed optional hardtops), a variety of engine tuning stages up to 600bhp, body and interior styling kits, and suspension, steering and braking modifications – all TUV-approved.

The leading Jaguar specialist in Germany, Arden also have many customers elsewhere, and subsidiaries in Japan and Switzerland carry out Arden conversions locally. Also, the company usually has an impressive presence at major international motor shows.

No XJR-S Convertibles were sold in the UK or Europe, but North America received a special batch of 50 (and just 50 Coupes) towards the end of XJR production. This left-hand-drive development XJR-S Convertible was photographed in 1992.

One of many items Arden have developed for the XJ-S: a detachable hardtop for the Convertible, made from Kevlar and equipped with a heated rear window.

Arden's rear-seat conversion for two-seater Convertibles; upholstery is in Connolly hide.

WP Automotive/Lister Cars

Laurence Pearce – son of the noted E-type racer of the Sixties, Warren Pearce – commenced modifying XJ-S Coupes around 1985 under the WP Automotive banner, both for the road and the race track. Increasingly competent and quick cars from Pearce's Leatherhead premises persuaded Brian Lister to allow him the use of his name, the new-generation 'Listers' produced from 1987 evoking memories of the almost unbeatable Lister-Jaguar sports-racing cars of the late 1950s.

By the time the Lister Mk 3 arrived in production in 1989, Laurence Pearce had developed his XJ-S into a formidable road sportscar, able to take on almost any Ferrari, as independent tests proved. A new 78.5mm long-stroke crankshaft machined from an EN40B steel billet gave 6.0 litres, and with larger valves, reprofiled camshafts, a special induction system with twin throttle bodies and a new Marelli digital ignition system, the engine produced a claimed 465bhp-plus and 420lb ft of torque. This was put through to the 3.54 Powr-Lok final-drive by a special AP clutch and an uprated Getrag five-speed manual gearbox.

The 1993 Lister Mk 3 Coupe; this is a 7.0-litre twin-supercharged car. You'd need an XJ220 to be quicker!

81

Naturally, the suspension was considerably beefed-up, and Pirelli 245/45 ZR16 P Zero tyres adorned three-piece alloy wheels, necessitating massive wheelarch extensions; power assistance was reduced and the steering geared to 2.5 turns lock to lock. Four-pot alloy calipers worked on 13.2in x 1.5in ventilated discs to provide impressive stopping power. Including a reworked leather interior with special sports seats, the coupe retailed for around £55,000.

From early 1989, a Convertible to a similar specification was offered at £73,000; the writer drove the first Mk 3 Convertible and recalls that wheelspin starts did not require dropping the clutch at high revs; simply depressing the accelerator with the car rolling in first gear did the trick! Road tests showed a 0–60mph time of around 5 seconds, with 100mph coming up in 12 seconds. A few Mk 3s made it to the United States, but mostly, it seems, without the engine modifications, due to Federal emission regulations.

While production of the Mk 3 continued, on April 11, 1989 the £121,000 'droop snoot' Lister Le Mans was launched and took over as the ultimate Lister XJ-S. It was charac-

The WP Automotive-developed 7.0-litre could be ordered with two superchargers, the one for the right-hand bank being visible here, down by the radiator.

The most radical Lister XJ-S was the Le Mans, its dropped nose aimed at better air penetration – and more individuality! This is a convertible example, photographed in 1991.

terized by a new sloping bonnet under which was an even more modified, 94 x 84mm, 6,996cc V12 unit giving a claimed (and believable) 496bhp at 6,200rpm. This made it one of the most powerful British cars ever offered. Wheel-rim widths were no less than 10in front and 13in rear, carrying 17in diameter Pirelli P Zeros, 245-section front and 335-section rear. Other chassis modifications were similar to those of the Mk 3. This projectile could reach 60mph in just 4.4 seconds and 100mph in 10.5 seconds – despite a special, full luxury interior.

The Convertible Le Mans arrived mid-1990, just about taking advantage of the tail-end of the performance/ luxury car boom (at £165,000 it needed to!). Engine and suspension modifications followed those of the Le Mans Coupe. Meanwhile, the Mk 3 continued in limited production and in 1993 it and the Le Mans were offered with twin superchargers and six gears… Power went up to a test-bed 540bhp and torque to 510lb ft, giving an estimated 190mph top speed. For a Mk 3, the complete conversion, including suspension, body and interior, cost £65,000 (you supplied the car). Pearce also sold individual performance parts and engine and manual transmission conversions.

In fact these exercises were but a step on the way to Laurence Pearce achieving his ambition to produce his own car, the extraordinary front-engined, four-seater Lister Storm, with a Jaguar V12-derived engine (one ran at XJ220C lap speeds at Le Mans in 1995, but that's another story!).

The very creditable total of some 150 Mk 3s and over 35 Le Mans versions were built – though as most cars were constructed to individual order, few were of exactly the same specification. Although WP Automotive Ltd fell foul of the supercar market collapse, Lister Cars effectively took their place and besides building the V12 Storm, still produced the Mk 3 (and upgraded Mk 4) while also offering their well-proven engine, transmission, suspension and brake conversions, plus various other enhancements to XJ-S owners.

So the Lister name continues to be associated with Jaguar-derived vehicles, and it is true to say that of all the privateer Jaguar performance specialists who addressed the XJ-S, Laurence Pearce was at their head with a blend of investment, engineering quality and marketing rare in the field.

Lynx Motors International

Established in 1971 to restore C-types and D-types, and producing D-type replicas from 1974, Lynx turned to a current-model Jaguar in 1980 when they announced the XJ-S Spyder. This was probably the first serious Coupe-to-Convertible conversion to be properly marketed; it featured an electrically-operated, lined mohair top, and the design retained the Coupe's rear seats. The Spyder was well-received, and production continued even after Jaguar introduced the Cabriolet, some customers preferring a full drophead. Only when the official Jaguar Convertible became available as a reasonably priced used car did the Spyder fade from Lynx's catalogues.

But by far the most popular Lynx XJ-S variant was – and is – the Eventer. Launched in 1983, this handsome 'estate' version of the XJ-S Coupe found a niche market amongst those who wanted a fast, stylish and fashionable load-carrier. It is also fair to say that the Eventer is probably the only privately restyled Jaguar that could pass muster as a factory original.

Conversions are carried out on new or used XJ-Ss of most specifications, though V12s have predominated, and by early 1996 the remarkable total of 63 Eventers had been sold.

Available many years before Jaguar produced an open XJ-S, the Lynx Spyder went on sale during 1980.

The Lynx Performer had a relatively short life, but its body styling was eye-catching and in turbocharged form its acceleration was awe-inspiring.

Unique in concept, the Lynx Eventer has justifiably enjoyed considerable success; this is the latest model with 'facelift' rear-end and concealed tailgate hinges. Half of the total built have gone to overseas customers. Besides possessing an enormous luggage area for a GT, the car also gives more room for rear-seat passengers.

Besides offering a potential 6ft long, 46cu ft luggage area with the rear seats folded, additional benefits include more legroom for rear passengers and better visibility.

As Jaguar developed the XJ-S, so did Lynx evolve their conversion to also suit successive new models, and Eventers can be produced from any type of XJ-S Coupe – though economics dictate that subject cars need to be less than five or six years old. The cost of an Eventer conversion was £21,500 (plus VAT if applicable) in 1996; earlier models can also be upgraded with such as 1995-specification moulded front and rear bumpers, and the latest horizontal rear lamp panel arrangement.

The Lynx Performer became available during the late 1980s in a number of guises, ranging from simply Lynx's exclusive body styling kit with its huge rear wing to a (literally) full-blown, turbocharged monster. The turbo conversion came in three stages, the ultimate L450 version extracting no less than 450bhp from the 4.0-litre AJ6 engine. A single Garret turbocharger was used, plus a remapped ECU, oil-cooled pistons giving a 6.5:1 compression ratio, gas-flowed cylinder head, and Wills rings to retain explosive cylinder pressures.

The conversion cost £11,000 and gave the 4.0-litre XJ-S an estimated 0–100mph time of little over 12 seconds. Suspension (including Lynx's well-proven A-frame rear suspension modification), brakes, steering and interior trim options were also available. Only a handful of fully-converted Performers were built, although the body kits proved popular and can still be seen occasionally on older XJ-Ss, though Lynx no longer market Performer parts or conversions.

Autostyle

Paul Banham has been attending to XJ-S owners' needs for a good number of years now, commencing with cosmetic touches, but now extending to a totally restyled bodyshell which looks like a cross between an E-type and a Ferrari, guaranteeing attention wherever it goes. Very popular has been Autostyle's 'wide body' conversion, endowing the XJ-S with mammoth wheelarch extensions to cover much wider wheels. A fixed-head model with longer side windows and no flying buttresses has also been developed.

Autostyle has evolved a successful Coupe-to-Convertible conversion, this also providing rear seats if required. More

Autostyle have completed many 'wide body' XJ-S conversions, some including the turning of Coupes into Convertibles. A GRP lift-off hardtop for the XJ-S Convertible is another Autostyle product. *(Illustration: Ian Cooling Collection)*

subtle are their interior embellishments, these including a replacement dashboard giving 'modern' round instruments throughout. Various wood veneers are also offered.

Autostyle are now one of Britain's most active companies in the aftermarket XJ-S field, and in common with other leading firms they attract a good deal of custom from Europe.

Paul Bailey Design

PBB Design was formed in 1987 by Paul Bailey, who in 1992 produced a spectacularly reskinned XJ-S Coupe; this was available with various suspension and powertrain options, including a 600bhp 7.0-litre V12 developed by Rob Beere Engineering (employing technology learned by Rob Beere while developing the racing V12 used by Malcolm Hamilton's all-conquering racing E-type).

Both steel and composites are used for the company's present £20,000 flagship, which boasts virtually all-new exterior panels. Those having less ambitious plans for their XJ-S can pick from a range of goodies, including three types of rear spoiler, four-headlamp conversions, vented bonnets, a horizontal rear lamp conversion, interior restyling and, of course, engine and suspension modifications.

The remarkable reclothing of an XJ-S Coupe by Paul Bailey aroused much interest when it was shown in the early 1990s.

Harvey-Bailey Engineering

One of the most competitive drivers of XK and E-type cars in the 1960s, Rhoddy Harvey-Bailey later established a company specializing in improving vehicle handling. HBE is now regarded as being a leader in its field and acts as consultant to many leading race teams, while also offering numerous (and effective) handling kits for road cars.

Available for the XJ-S are matched sets of replacement anti-roll bars and dampers, carefully developed to improve roadholding and handling without destroying the car's innately good ride qualities. HBE also offer their own design of front underside cross-bracing for earlier XJ-S Convertibles, considerably reducing scuttle shake, and a rear suspension anti-tramp frame for all XJ-S models.

Hyper

Intentionally catering for those who could or would not afford more exotic offerings, since the late 1980s Paul Hands has offered a variety of modifications for the XJ-S and, in the autumn of 1988, most of these were encapsulated in the Hands Hyper S. This featured suspension, steering and brake modifications, plus a unique modification to the automatic gearbox which eliminated the automatic change – the selection of ratios was entirely driver-controlled through the selector lever. There was even an overdrive conversion giving the GM box four speeds.

The complete conversion, including a four-piece body kit, sold for £7,000, but in common with many non-official aftermarket offerings, few cars were built to exactly the same specification. Individual parts and kits were and are still available, as well as complete cars. Now based at the same Kidlington trading estate from which JaguarSport Ltd used to operate, Hands continues to offer parts, services and modifications for XJ-S cars.

In 1984 engineering director Jim Randle evolved a longer-wheelbase XJ-S Coupe; the extra 4 inches were accommodated behind the door and markedly increased legroom. A remodelled top dispensed with the buttresses. The idea was not proceeded with, but the car survives. The modified Coupe was produced in experimental Daimler form, too, with appropriate badging and fluted number-plate finisher.

CHAPTER 8

XJ-S on the track

Works-backed teams on both sides of the Atlantic

Group 44

Bob Tullius and his eastern United States-based Group 44 team had already played a key role boosting Jaguar's sporting image and sales in the United States, having secured a national championship with their modified V12 E-type in 1975. Tullius continued to field the now-obsolete roadster during the first part of 1976, but the same year he had little difficulty in persuading Jaguar's US bosses, Graham Whitehead and Mike Dale, that the team should switch to the latest sporting Jaguar, the XJ-S. They in turn persuaded British Leyland – within which Jaguar then operated – that a successful showing on the track would elevate both Jaguar's and British Leyland's image in the USA.

So Group 44 made ready to contest the Sports Car Club of America's highly competitive TransAm production sportscar series. It was the first fully professional series which Group 44, founded in 1965 by Robert Tullius and engineer/driver Brian Fuerstenau, had tackled, and even the confident Tullius was initially a little overawed.

But at least in turning the soft and comfortable XJ-S into a proper racer Group 44 could draw on their considerable experience preparing the Series 3 E-type – which, of course, had a similar power unit and rear suspension. Unlike Broadspeed with the ill-starred XJ12C project (underway at the same time in England), Fuerstenau elected to stay with as many stock Jaguar components as possible; certainly he considered the V12 engine's crankshaft and connecting rods to be perfectly up to the job. He did, however, design a dry-sump lubrication system – as with the similarly equipped Jaguar D-type of many years before, this was mainly to provide a larger reservoir of oil for long-distance racing. Also, being more familiar with carburation than fuel injection, he installed six twin-choke Webers. The power output of the original 1976-specification engine was quoted as 475bhp at 7,600rpm.

Nor was the chassis modified out of recognition; the rear brakes remained inboard (though larger discs were fitted front and rear) and the basic suspension geometry was not altered dramatically. The regulations allowed certain bodywork modifications, however, and Group 44 were able to fit much wider alloy wheels and slick racing tyres.

The XJ-S's first race was not until August, when, at Mosport, Ontario, Tullius finished fourth in Category 1 against such as the Chevrolet Camaro and Porsche 911. The car's first win came at the next outing, at Lime Rock, and although the two other races contested that season were marred by minor faults, the potential of the Group 44-prepared XJ-S was obvious. Certainly Tullius himself was impressed by the car, including its aerodynamics, and described how at Daytona he could "drive up and down the banking at 180mph quite effortlessly".

In 1977, Group 44 competed in the Sports Car Club of America's TransAm series, travelling many thousands of miles to run at circuits all over North America and Canada. Of six hours' duration, the longest race had been at Mosport, and Tullius, sharing the driving with Fuerstenau, took the gleaming white XJ-S to victory – Jaguar's first long-distance success since the Mk 2 3.8 saloon's swansong win in New Zealand back in 1966. Some 10 races were contested in all, with Tullius winning Category 1 five times and accumulating enough points to give him the Drivers' Championship in his division. 'Thundering elegance' was the emotive phrase used in Jaguar's advertising as they made the most out of the victory.

That winter, the original car (2W51120) was further modified, while an entirely new car was also built up for the 1978 TransAm season. Again, 10 races were involved, the old car competing alongside the new in two of them, driven by Fuerstenau.

At Sears Point, California, Tullius was delayed by other people's accidents and came ninth; at Westwood, British Columbia, he improved to second; at Portland, Oregon, he was third; St Jovite, near Montreal, brought the first Category 1 win of the season; and at the six-hours Watkins Glen, New York State race, the XJ-S again finished first, driven by Tullius and Fuerstenau. At Mosport, Ontario, Tullius secured third; at Brainerd, Minnesota, he won again – and his victory at Road America, Wisconsin, ensured that he could not be beaten in the Driver's Championship. Tullius dominated again at Laguna Seca, California, where Fuerstenau came third in

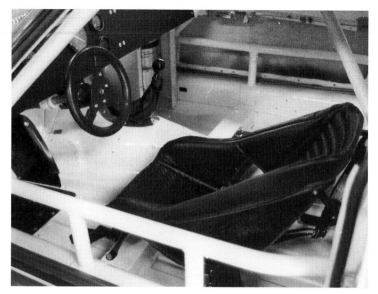

Cockpit of the 1976 car: a basically standard bodyshell was used, but the dash and all trim were removed; the driver was protected (and the shell braced) by substantial roll-over and side-intrusion bars.

The further-developed Group 44 XJ-S, photographed in July 1977 at Watkins Glen, where it finished fourth. Note the European-style lamp panel – and the screen decal acknowledging that Jaguar was still within British Leyland... *(Photo: Jaguar Cars Inc Archive)*

The 'bodyshell' car backed-up the new tubular-framed machine when the XJ-S returned to the TransAm series in 1981.

the original car; and finally, in the Copa Mexico TransAm, Mexico City, Tullius again won to also secure the Manufacturers' Championship for Jaguar. He could hardly have done better!

While the Group 44 Jaguars did not compete in 1979 and 1980, the XJ-S racing story in the United States was not over yet, for Graham Whitehead – and John Egan – sanctioned the return of the XJ-S to motor racing in 1981. This time, outright victories would be sought; SCCA rules now allowed spaceframed 'silhouette' cars and a suitably redesigned XJ-S seemed to offer much promise.

Redesigned it certainly was: there was no pretence at using an original shell, and instead there was a tubular frame clad with non-structural lightweight XJ-S lookalike panels. Now developing some 525bhp (or, "off the record, nearer 550" as Bob Tullius told me at the time!), the V12 engine was 7½in further back to put more weight over the rear wheels. Group 44-made wishbone suspension front and rear carried the even wider wheels.

A quick-change Franklin differential replaced the Salisbury

unit and, in fact, the whole car was built not only for lightness and strength (the latter always a Tullius priority), but for quick and easy replacement of even major components should it prove necessary at the circuit. This was a policy that paid off several times, enabling the XJ-S to be brought to the grid after earlier problems might have sidelined other cars.

The 1981 season began well at Charlotte, North Carolina, with a second place for the new car, followed by an outright win at Portland. Electrical problems spoiled the next two outings, then Tullius won at Brainerd. An uncharacteristic timing chain breakage halted the XJ-S at Trois Rivieres, Quebec, but at Mosport it was the turn of series leader Eppie Wietzes' Corvette to suffer engine problems and the Jaguar won. At Laguna Seca, California, the XJ-S developed gearbox trouble and Tullius finished fifth, and although George Follmer's Camaro won, Weitzes' third place gave him the Championship. At the ninth and last race, at Sears Point, the XJ-S ran strongly until gear selection became difficult and Tullius retired. A Mustang won.

Thus Group 44 had to settle for second in the TransAm

The tubular-framed XJ-S which very nearly gained the TransAm Championship with outright wins in 1981.

Championship; but this was no disgrace with a very new car against experienced and equally professional competition, especially as the tubular-framed car's three wins had brought Group 44's total XJ-S victory tally up to 29 between 1977 and 1981, a remarkable achievement.

The 1981 TransAm car was to compete one more time as Bob Tullius entered it in the Daytona 24 Hours race early in 1982; co-drivers were Bill Adam and Gordon Smiley. But that was simply to test the V12 engine over a full 24 hours of competition, something difficult to simulate on an engine dynometer. Why? Because Tullius, Group 44 and Jaguar were moving on to greater things still: GT prototype endurance racing with their new scratch-built mid-engined XJR-5, to be powered by essentially the same Jaguar V12 power unit that the team had used since 1975.

As a test-session the Daytona 24 Hours was fine, though the car's run was interrupted by problems due to a rogue set of gears in the long-suffering but normally reliable Jaguar four-speed production gearbox (this, somewhat amazingly, had coped remarkably well with up to 550bhp over the five seasons the team had raced Jaguars).

The engine itself ran perfectly for 26 hours, including practice. "Then, when we got home, we took it out of the car and used it as a mule on the dyno for 10 hours, and it was still perfect" recounted Bob afterwards. More surprisingly, Bob also revealed: "We attained a speed of 194.46mph at Daytona – on street tyres!" It had been team supplier Goodyear who suggested the XJ-S be run on road tyres for the event; they worked fine – fortunately...

But for the untimely death of driver Gordon Smiley at Indianapolis in May 1982, the XJ-S might have contested one more TransAm Championship as Smiley had negotiated sponsorship which would have enabled him to have taken over the car from Group 44. On his death, though, the car was retired for good.

Group 44's efforts with the XJ-S had been magnificent and had considerably upgraded Jaguar's image both through the late 1970s 'valley of the shadow' through to 1981, when Jaguar – and the XJ-S – were on the verge of an amazing revival. But now, the XJ-S racing torch would be taken up by a British team.

TWR

While Ralph Broad's racing XJ12C project of 1976/77 had been supported by British Leyland in the hope that it would enhance the whole BL range, the idea had been regarded with grave misgivings by Jaguar. These feelings were amply justified by events: although the coupes had shown enormous speed, they did not win a single race during the two seasons they were campaigned. But by the early 1980s a different set of circumstances emerged: new European Touring Car regulations were coming into effect which would suit the XJ-S very well, and Jaguar, now led by John Egan and on its way to privatization, was receptive to schemes which would raise the company's profile.

Jaguar engineering had in fact spent some time secretly investigating the XJ-S for racing within a year of the car being launched. But any lingering thoughts of direct factory

involvement in competition were dropped after it was finally accepted that motor racing, even where production cars were concerned, was now so specialized that only an outside, dedicated team could develop a potential race-winning car and thereafter continue to keep pace with the opposition.

Tom Walkinshaw's approach to Jaguar in 1981 with a plan to race the XJ-S was therefore timely. He had already proved himself as driver and team manager with BMW, Mazda and Rover touring cars, and the new Group A regulations scheduled for the European Touring Car Championship in 1982 appeared ideal for the XJ-S – which just qualified as a touring car by dint of its 'plus-2' seating.

So there followed an exploratory season in which TWR was covertly backed by Jaguar on a 'see what you can do' basis. Running first one, then two cars, the team showed great promise, winning four ETC races – at Brno, Nurburgring, Silverstone and Zolder. So for 1983 Tom Walkinshaw received formal support and began the season with two newly-liveried cars running as the TWR Jaguar team. Their chief rival was now the BMW-backed 635CSi 3.5-litre coupe, just homolo-

The first, black and red, Motul-sponsored XJ-S of 1982, photographed at the Donington ETC round by Chris Harvey.

Motul remained a sponsor for 1983, the French oil company finding worthwhile exposure on the Continent as the ETC circus moved around. Here the TWR-Jaguars dominate the grid at Donington in May.

The engine bay of the 1983 TWR XJ-S, showing ducting taking cold air to the intake. Over 400bhp was produced from the 5.3-litre V12.

gated and more of a match for the 5.3-litre V12 Jaguars than the 528i saloon which had run in 1982.

With the regulations insisting that wheels and tyres remained within the original bodywork, the Group A XJ-S's appearance remained remarkably true to its roadgoing sisters. But much had changed under the skin. TWR managed to hide 17in rim, 13in wide, Speedline alloy wheels under the arches, the rear suspension was much modified with new, very wide, fabricated lower wishbones (augmented not by trailing arms, but by a strong 'A' bracket), while outboard brakes took the heat away from the differential.

As braking and transmission were unrestricted, AP four-pot calipers and larger discs were used all round, and originally, Jaguar's own four-speed gearbox was used, later replaced by the Getrag five-speed unit. Within the limitations imposed by the regulations on valves and lift, the Lucas-injected 5.3-litre V12 was modified extensively and gave 400bhp-plus.

Walkinshaw and Belgian driver/journalist Pierre Dieudonne put the two XJ-S Coupes, resplendent in a new, predominantly white, paint scheme, on the front row of the grid at Monza for the first round of 1983. They were ahead of no less than 10 635CSi BMWs, and it looked like a secure Jaguar victory until a loose bonnet necessitated a pitstop. The race – and, as it turned out at the end of the season, the 1983 Championship – was lost by just 3½ seconds.

Vallelunga produced a third place, and then it was back to England and the Donington 500 in May; John Fitzpatrick and the young Martin Brundle were now in the team, and it was Brundle who, in an enthralling dash through torrential rain, wound in Dieter Quester's BMW and won by 20 seconds.

Later the same month, Walkinshaw and 'Chuck Nicholson' won at Pergusa, third was secured at Mugello, and a win at Brno saw Walkinshaw take the lead in the Championship, consolidated by a Jaguar one-two at the Osterreichring. Then came the Nurburgring six-hours race, the last such International to be held over the original, daunting old circuit. Alas, as with too many Jaguars of the past, the Ring's crests and leaps caused mechanical havoc and both cars retired. Just Walkinshaw's fastest lap remained as a consolation.

Next, at the Salzburgring, a lone XJ-S vanquished the BMWs, but then bad luck set in. At Spa, the duration was over the full 24 hours; one XJ-S retired with differential failure and the other with a large-scale engine blow-up; but they had led at one stage, and 12 of the 16 BMW coupes entered also failed to finish.

Then the home crowd was disappointed when, at Silverstone in July, the team could manage no better than ninth, handicapped in the wet conditions by unsuitable tyres. At least the race was won by a British car – a Rover SD1 V8, also prepared by TWR.

Walkinshaw just needed to finish fourth or higher in the final round at Zolder, Belgium. Win Percy, indeed, led the race, but then retired with clutch failure, while Brundle struggled in the other XJ-S with a recalcitrant gearchange. This sorted itself out, but despite his, Walkinshaw's and Percy's best efforts they ended the race eighth. The title went to a delighted Quester in the 635CSi, BMW winning six races to runner-up Jaguar's five.

While the 1984 ETC saw the emergence of much more competitive, turbocharged, Volvos, it was again to be basically a Jaguar *versus* BMW fight. In March, Jaguar announced that a three-car team would be competing this time, and that Hans Heyer, Quester's 1983 partner, would be Tom Walkinshaw's co-driver. The other pilots were 1983 men Win Percy, 'Chuck Nicholson', Martin Brundle and the Swiss, Enzo Calderari.

All began well: although one car was sidelined when it shed belts, Walkinshaw and Heyer sliced through the rain to win by 7sec from Kelleners' BMW. Still in Italy, the same two drivers secured third in a bitty race at Vallelunga, and at Donington, the locals had something to cheer about when Percy and 'Nicholson' took the chequered flag.

On to Spain and the XJ-Ss posted a storming one-two-three at Pergusa – then repeated it at Brno, Walkinshaw himself gaining his third successive victory at the Czechoslovakian circuit. David Sears had joined the team by then (his father Jack was a fine sportscar driver from a former era, with plenty of Jaguar drives to his name).

In Austria it wasn't quite total domination as a failed engine meant that the TWR Jaguar team took 'only' the first two places. The Nurburgring jinx struck again when the ETC circus went to Germany, even though the new circuit was but a shadow of the magnificent original. A series of mechanical misfortunes kept the Jaguars out of the lead, though Walkinshaw did a stint in the fifth-placed XJ-S to add more useful points to his Championship total.

At Spa-Francorchamps, things went better. Walkinshaw decided to run only two cars, one shared by himself, Hans Heyer and Win Percy, the other by Calderari, Sears and Belgian Teddy Pilette. If the Jaguar fans present were initially dismayed when the Jaguars played second-fiddle to the BMWs, they needn't have worried – 24 hours is a long time, and Tom was determined to pace his cars carefully.

The Saturday was mainly wet and the BMWs took an early lead, but during the night, and after some 12 hours racing, one mud-streaked Jaguar was out in front, even if the Calderari car had retired after hitting the Armco. Building up a three-lap cushion, the lone XJ-S despatched the laps with clockwork precision and a Jaguar won a major 24-hours race for the first time since 1957 – in the week when Jaguar shares

Rear suspension of the 1984 XJ-S showing TWR's strong, fabricated lower wishbones. Also seen is the on-board hydraulic jacking system, which saved vital seconds during pitstops.

were put on the market as the company cut free from BL.

By contrast, the Tourist Trophy round at Silverstone was a disaster, the TWR Jaguar team making an uncharacteristic tactical mistake when heavy rain suddenly fell by not bringing cars in immediately for wet tyres. Spins and possibly rain-induced engine problems meant that a certain win was thrown away, though Calderari and Sears finished second.

So the Championship, which could have been sewn up in Walkinshaw's favour there and then, was still open; but third place at Zolder was enough and Walkinshaw was confirmed as ETC Driver's Champion with 181 points. Team-mate Heyer was second with 171 points, comfortably ahead of the BMW and Alfa drivers. The final ETC race of 1984 was something of a formality, therefore, so two of the three Jaguars failing to finish was of no real importance.

Overall it had been a hard-fought but magnificent season for the TWR Jaguar team, vanquishing BMW in the over-2.5-litre class and securing the Driver's Championship (through consistent class wins, Alfa Romeo won the Manufacturers' Championship). On virtually every circuit the XJ-S had been able to circulate quicker than any other car, reliability had been excellent and the team organization and pitwork generally superb. It more than expunged the bad memories of the earlier Broadspeed effort and boosted Jaguar's – and the XJ-S's – reputation worldwide.

There was just one more race before the season ended: repainted in black and gold for a one-off John Player Special sponsorship deal, two XJ-Ss headed for Macau and the traditional November Grand Prix meeting. There, too, were a couple of Schnizter BMW 635CSi coupes and a mixed bag of mostly Japanese cars, but the Jaguars dominated the 95-mile event, with Tom Walkinshaw winning, ahead of Hans Heyer in the second XJ-S.

That sparkling 1984 season was to be last contested by a fully-fledged XJ-S works-backed team in Europe, but 1985 did bring a further significant victory and one which was particularly satisfying for Tom Walkinshaw – and for veteran Australian racing driver John Goss.

Touring car racing has always been important in Australia, with Jaguars figuring strongly in the 1960s when, right up to 1965, the Mk 2 saloon was kept competitive by local teams and drivers – big-engined V8 Holdens and Falcons notwithstanding. Of all the Australian circuits, Mount Panorama, at Bathurst, three hours' drive from Sydney, was by far the most spectacular, and in 1984 John Goss – who had achieved the unique double of winning the Australian GP and the 1000km James Hardie race at Bathurst – persuaded Tom Walkinshaw to co-drive with him there. The car was Goss' own XJ-S, a model he had run at Bathurst in 1980, 1981 and 1982, alas without success.

In 1984, the clutch had failed on the line, but Walkinshaw was sufficiently motivated to commit TWR to a full team effort for the following year's event, which was to be run to Group A rules for the first time. Three of the TWR-Jaguar team cars started in the October 1985 race.

A 24-hours victory! Best result of the 1984 season was undoubtedly the TWR Jaguar's win at Spa.

Soon, Jeff Allam was out from engine damage caused by the freak ingestion of, it appears, a piece of broken glass. That left Walkinshaw and Goss lying first and second, until the Walkinshaw/Percy car was afflicted by a broken oil cooler, which dropped it to 11th place. Although TW charged through the field to an eventual third place after repairs, it was now down to Goss and Armin Hahne to carry the Jaguar flag. In a battle to overcome the handicap of a driver's seat increasingly intent on freedom, Hahne and Goss did indeed take the chequered flag after 163 laps and 6 hours 41½ minutes – just 47.7 seconds ahead of the Schnitzer BMW 635CSi of Ravaglia and Cecotto (sponsored by former Jaguar saloon champion driver Bob Jane). It was a moment of undiluted personal triumph for Goss, and a great tribute to the TWR XJ-S which, on top of the Spa 24 Hours race, could now add victory in another of the world's greatest touring car races to its tally.

Although one car was sold to a collector, Tom Walkinshaw found opportunities for several more outings. He obtained sponsorship to take two cars to Japan in November 1986, but while the two XJ-Ss initially dominated the five-hour Group A race at Fuji, engine failure and an (unusual) axle failure meant the cars didn't finish. Perhaps the most interesting aspect of this race was that former F1 World Champion, New Zealander Denny Hulme, partnered Armin Hahne in the second XJ-S and proved extremely quick, overtaking everything except the leading Volvo turbo.

There was no real possibility of the XJ-S returning to European touring car racing the following year as the car's homologation ran out at the end of 1986, and the 1987 regulations demanded greater rear seat depth. Yet such was the attraction of the TWR XJ-S that the organizers of New Zealand's four-hour race at Wellington in January 1987 extended Group A homologation for a month to allow the Jaguars two final excursions.

The Wellington event did not go well; Armin Hahne went off the track, and Win Percy's car also retired, apparently due

Win Percy and 'Chuck Nicholson' brought home the bacon at Donington in April 1984.

The XJ-S of Walkinshaw and Heyer at Donington, though it was the Percy/'Nicholson' car that would win.

to differential failure again. Just one TWR Jaguar appeared on the grid at Pukekohe in February 1987, driven by Percy and Hahne, who completed the Group A XJ-S's career with a good second place behind the Holden Commodore of Perkins and Hulme. Competitive to the end, even though, with only a couple of races undertaken, further development over the previous two years must have been modest.

All in all, the TWR XJ-S had brought Jaguar 20 outright wins and much positive exposure, while in the marketplace it greatly raised the credibility of the XJ-S as a true sporting car. Tom Walkinshaw, of course, went on to mastermind the TWR-Jaguar team's attack on the World Sports Car Championship, garnering two Jaguar Le Mans victories in the process, while also establishing a strong Jaguar presence in the USA's IMSA race series.

Seven different XJ-S Coupes were raced over the duration of the ETC programme. All were owned by TWR and all except one were sold off to private owners. No 1, the original

red and black car of 1982, has long been in a private museum in the US, as has No 2, the first of the white/green stripe 1983 cars, and presumably the second 1982 car. No 3, the second 1983-season car, is in private ownership in the UK, has been repainted in green 1984 colours (and is possibly the only example to have been made road-legal!).

Also remaining in the UK at the time of writing (early 1996) are the green/white stripe 1984 cars, Nos 4, 5 and 6. The latter is one of the few to return to racing, owner Allen Lloyd occasionally driving it spiritedly in British Historic Group 1 events (John Goss, of Bathurst fame, owns a genuine TWR lightweight bodyshell, but this is unnumbered in the above sequence, while the Jaguar Daimler Heritage Trust keeps another unnumbered, unmodified car cosmetically prepared in 1984 team colours for exhibition purposes).

As for No 7, the 1984 European Championship-winning XJ-S, and the car that won most races, that's remained securely in Tom Walkinshaw's personal collection!

CHAPTER 9

Assessment and purchase

Choices and characters

So you fancy buying an XJ-S! Not too difficult an ambition to achieve, you might think – after all, there are plenty advertised, at least in the UK and the US. But it's not quite that simple because the XJ-S was in production for over 20 years and there are a bewildering number of models and sub-models, embracing three different body styles and four different engine capacities.

The situation is made all the more complex through Jaguar's habit of bringing in a multiplicity of individual changes on the XJ-S over a period of time, rather than packaging them together in a few distinct, easily-defined new models. This approach was forced upon Jaguar by a lack of money and resources; as previous chapters have chronicled, there was a plethora of both visual and engineering upgrades, especially during the last five or six years of the car's life, spawning full, '½' and even '¾' model-year variants, some with new front-ends, some with redesigned rear-ends, some with 4.0-litre engines and some with new bumpers. Yet the substance of these changes had in the most part been designed way back in the mid-1980s, and many could have arrived all together…

At least it provides the would-be XJ-S buyer with choice, and there should be a model to suit every taste, need and bank balance. Obviously, quoting prices in a book which will (hopefully!) have long-term currency is inappropriate as the majority of cars are still depreciating; all one can say is that good, low-mileage, pre-1988 cars will probably drop no further. Current price barometers include the club magazines, the bookstall title *Jaguar World*, and for late-model cars the various price guides found in any major newsagent. An alter-native is to befriend your local Jaguar specialist; many tend to have their fingers on the pulse of market values. Certainly the potential price range in 1996 was enormous, spanning £1,500 to £50,000 in the UK, according to the car's age, type and condition.

But let's disregard money for a moment and look at character. The very first, pre-HE cars are dramatically different from later models in the way they drive, especially the final sporting versions of the 1990s. Slip into the low, soft driving seat of a 1976 car, put the ignition key into the austere black dashboard and grasp the big, skinny, black steering wheel, and before you even drive off you know you are in a different world from that of the mid-1990s XJS, with its chunky sports seats, thick-rimmed steering wheel and copious areas of veneer.

Move off and you find the need to adopt an altogether different driving style, too; the original XJ-S was built for speed, but in an understated way. The accent was on effortless cruising, relying on the power of that magnificent V12 to waft you from corner to corner without the need to achieve high averages by invoking ungentlemanly-high 'g' forces *round* the corners; true Grand Touring in the original prewar sense of the term. The XJ-S is still a fast car today, but I can tell you that in 1975 an ability to cruise at 130mph in near-silence, with virtually another 20mph in reserve, was awe-inspiring. Combined with immense acceleration, it put you into a different time-sphere to other road-users, who appeared almost to be stationary objects around which the XJ-S effortlessly wove.

Mind you, when it came to corners the steering on those early cars was (and is) so light and the steering rack mount-

The original XJ-S concept discarded mid-engined configurations – and the two-seater sportscar approach of its forebears, the XK 120, XK 150 and E-Type, seen here in this 1975 photograph. Instead it embraced a Grand Tourer image. *Photo P Skilleter*

The car that saved the XJ-S: the HE model, which was introduced in July 1981, with its less thirsty V12 engine and new wood veneer interior, reversed the car's downward sales spiral. This is a 1984 example. *Photo P Skilleter*

find that the 20-year-old machine's handling is both predictable and fun, allowing unexpectedly high cross-country averages to be maintained.

Its 205-section Dunlops plus quite soft springing and damping can't provide the outright grip of a later car – for sheer roadholding ability a late 4.0-litre Sports-suspended, wide-wheeled Coupe has to be the ultimate XJ-S – but the trade-off gives a serenity of ride, especially at low speeds, that was lost as the XJ-S was modernized with stiff, low-profile rubber and firmer damping.

Indeed, transport a 1975 XJ-S driver through time and send him or her down the road in a 6.0-litre Sports XJ-S and they would be shocked at the car's knobbly ride quality around town; just as they would be amazed by its reserves of grip on a twisty road. Conversely, take owners of the late XJS back to 1975 and they could not fail to be impressed by the original car's superb low-speed ride, if a little bemused by its lackadaisical steering response and a certain absence of body control at high speed.

While condition is probably more important to most people than detail specification, the real sports enthusiast will be tempted to seek out the rare (352 built) four-speed manual gearbox car, which does add a new dimension to XJ-S driving. Or, if you want the best-performing early car, look for one of the digitally-injected 'flying machines' of late 1979/80.

The HE charts a serene middle course. Just a little tauter all round to give more precise steering and better body control, it kept to relatively 'tall'-section tyres and retains the effortless, gliding feel of the earlier car – and with no suggestion of the annoying 'tramlining' effect apparent with some of the later wide-tyred XJSs. Assuming door seals are good, refinement is better than that of its predecessor and not far off that of a late car. All this, combined with (at last) traditional Jaguar wood-and-leather, plus a less pronounced thirst, convince many that the HE is the best all-round XJ-S.

Of course, there were downsides. There was no manual gearbox option, so the marvellous flexibility of the V12 could not be exploited, and it took a little while for Egan's troubleshooting teams to achieve really acceptable build quality.

One person who was attracted to the model, even though he

Opposite ends: original 'gothic'-style rear lights contrast with the slick and feintly American treatment of the final cars' horizontal units. Tailpipes went from round to oval.

ings so relatively soft that you almost need to anticipate a bend and start turning the wheel before actually entering it: there's none of the perhaps too-instant turn-in of the later Sports pack cars. But it's something you rapidly acclimatize to, caressing the wheel with your finger-tips rather than grasping it firmly, Grand Prix driver-style – whereupon you

1975 facia is somewhat austere while the barrel instruments were never really liked: "pure BL Marina", said some of the interior, but the 70s look strikes a chord with early-car enthusiasts today.

knew that its limits on passenger and luggage space ruled out the XJ-S for long-term ownership, was my publisher, John Blunsden, who decided to run one for a year "to get it out of my system". I asked him to comment on his experiences:

"Like most of my colleagues at the press launch of the XJ-S, I was somewhat dismayed when the wraps came off the car for the first time. It wasn't that its shape was unattractive, just that we had been expecting something so very different. However, when the opportunity came to road-test the car, any reservations about the styling, or even the packaging, were quickly overpowered by the sheer exhilaration of being behind the wheel.

"I think I decided there and then that one day – when secondhand values brought the car within my reach – I would find a way to put an XJ-S in my garage. The feeling was reinforced over the years whenever I tested a later model, and the opportunity came towards the end of 1988, when I was offered a 1984 HE at what at the time seemed a very attractive price. I knew it was not the most appropriate car for my needs, but it did represent an incredible amount of car for the

money, so I decided I would run it for a year, then revert to something with more passenger and luggage space.

"It was a memorable year, one that I have never regretted. On the plus side there was the massive torque from that silky V12 engine (and what a masterpiece of plumbing there was beneath the bonnet!); the feeling that all the mechanical components were so wonderfully understressed; the effortless performance that came with just a little more pressure from the right foot; the games one could play with the trip computer, proving that skilled use of the accelerator could effect dramatic – and necessary! – improvements in fuel consumption without any real detriment to journey times.

"On the negative side, yes, if I accelerated hard and ran the engine at anything close to its full potential I paid a heavy price on the fuel gauge, and of course with all that weight up front it was wise to brake early before roundabouts in order to retain a reasonable disc pad life. The lightness of the steering took some getting used to, although after a time it ceased to worry me, and ground clearance was a touch marginal for crossing steeply cambered road gutters and pavements.

A new badge, a new engine capacity: the XJ-S coupe launched the AJ6 engine in October 1983; coupled to a five-speed manual gearbox and offering a 25mpg potential, the XJ-S 3.6 soon found many friends. *Photo P Skilleter*

Open-air motoring returned to Jaguar's sports range with the cabriolet, seen here in later V12 form. Something of a stopgap model, the cabriolet filled a niche until the true convertible XJ-S arrived. *Photo: Jaguar Cars*

The Cabriolet – this is a special Burberry plaid-trimmed example from 1984 (VIN 116005) – it has somewhat idiosyncratic roofing arrangements, but possesses real charm and the kudos of comparative rarity.

"During my year-and-a-bit of ownership I must have covered something in excess of 12,000 miles with just one technical hiccup – without any prior warning, a fuel pump went on the blink, necessitating a somewhat apprehensive 40-mile journey back to my local Jaguar agency, where it was promptly replaced.

"Notwithstanding this inconvenience, I never felt that the engineering quality and robustness of the XJ-S's major mechanical components were a cause for any concern, but I was less happy with the detail quality – the fit and the finish – of what we might call the cosmetics. For example, the first time it happened it seemed quite amusing that one of the two dashboard-mounted interior lights fell out of its housing when I shut the door, but like most jokes, the more frequently it was repeated the more difficult it became to laugh at it. The flimsy fixing arrangements were the cause, and a closer look at all the car's detail equipment provided evidence for me of where some of the pennies had been saved.

"Fortunately, at least some of (Sir) John Egan's admirable efforts to improve the detail quality of Jaguars had benefited this particular car (the paint finish, for example, was excellent apart from two very small surface rust patches, which were easily made good), but this was an on-going process, and I'm sure that the younger the model, the less cause there should be for an owner to criticize the quality of its finish and fit.

"As for 'my' XJ-S, I parted with it with considerable regret, for it had given me a year's motoring of a very special quality at a surprisingly affordable cost. Interestingly, the couple to whom I sold it, and who several months later told me that they were still delighted with it, also said that they had been attracted to ownership of an XJ-S in the first place because it really did seem to represent an awful lot of car for the money. That, of course, has always been one of its great attractions."

It was the 3.6 Coupe of 1983 that marked the XJ-S's first radical character-change when it attempted to be a sportscar for the first time. With a manual gearbox behind the engine once more and tauter suspension, the transition was largely successful – though many of us were taken aback by the raucousness of the new AJ6 engine as originally installed. Fortunately, this was sorted out, leaving the 3.6 with many unalloyed virtues; the choice of five speeds made up much of the power deficit compared with the V12 and its three-speed sludge-stirrer, though the five-plane Getrag was a mite clumsy; while – miracle! – here was an XJ-S that could achieve up to 25mpg! An important factor today if you intend to cover a fair annual mileage.

Then there are the open-top cars: if you can tolerate the slightly fussy roof-opening operations, the Cabriolet has much to offer. It allows various open or partly open configurations and, in closed form, gives in essence a Coupe with better visibility and no flying buttresses.

Some actually prefer Cabriolet to Convertible, the former's permanent roof framing giving a measure of both roll-over protection and greater rigidity – early Convertibles did suffer from scuttle shake, which is much less acceptable now than it was in 1988. Others love the true Convertible's clean, sleek outline and the convenience of the power top (even if fitting the hood envelope can be something of a struggle).

The 4.0-litre, either Coupe or Convertible, is a cracking car. Especially in later, AJ16-engined form, the straight-six is virtually as refined as the V12, especially at high rpm (indeed, I reckon a good 4.0-litre can actually be superior in this respect). Its extra power over the 3.6 closes the performance gap, too, and if you add in the manual five-speed gearbox, away from motorways it is probably a quicker, more agile car than the heavier, automatic-transmission V12 – including the four-speed 6.0-litre variety. Mind you, the 'switchable' ZF automatic box is a delight, too, and probably adds to driving pleasure for most people.

As for the later V12s, in touring suspension form they nearly (but not quite) match the first XJ-S in terms of low-speed ride quality and swift, undemanding progress. They also possess many modern conveniences and gadgetry, while heating and ventilation systems and controls are so much better in late cars of any engine type. Fitted with Sports suspension, the car gains precision, but loses some of that famed Jaguar serenity; you take your choice, which is the beauty of the XJ-S buying game. The point must be made, however, that even the last XJ-Ss are by today's standards old-fashioned in many respects – visibility and cockpit space, for

Shunned by the mainstream trade secondhand, the XJR-S is a car of towering abilities and is now available at bargain prices.

The graceful XJ-S V12 convertible of 1988 was considerably more practical than the cabriolet it replaced, and its success in the United States surprised even Jaguar. *Photo: P Skilleter*

The JaguarSport XJR-S 6.0-litre in its revised 1992 model year form, with more integrated body fairings and revised interior. *Photo: P Skilleter*

example. By 1996 we could see that its successor was needed.

When it comes to straight-line acceleration, as different ignition, injection and engine management systems interacted first with non-catalyst and then with catalyst specifications, V12 performance varied over the years and late cars are not necessarily the quickest. In short, more sophisticated engine management plus – eventually – extra cubic capacity, just about produced the full circle, with the final, catalyst 6.0-litre automatic Coupe returning performance figures very similar to those of the original 1975 car… But there were degrees in between, as previous chapters have relayed; for example, a V12 high-point is the Marelli-ignited 'pre-cat' era of around 1989/90.

Remember that all V12 Jaguars are thirsty, and not even an HE will return much more than 12–14mpg around town with cold starts, and maybe up to 18–20mpg or a little more with reasonably sedate driving on long runs. OK if you don't intend to cover high mileages; otherwise, unless you have a deep pocket, a 'six' may be the car for you.

What of the JaguarSport models? Strangely, perhaps, they are slightly in limbo. Undoubtedly rare in either 5.3 or 6.0-litre forms compared to the standard XJ-S V12, yet they command little or no price premium and in the mid-1990s Jaguar main dealers tended to avoid stocking even the best and latest used examples. Some owners of earlier XJR-Ss even reported that their local Jaguar dealer denied the official existence of their car!

But it's an ill wind; lack of interest from the trade has resulted in relatively low prices, and this, combined with rarity and what most qualified observers rate as the best XJ-S chassis ever made, surely makes the XJR-S – especially in 6.0-litre form – a tremendous bargain for the right person. Prices will continue to go down for some time, but who knows? One day a genuine TWR, Le Mans Celebration or XJR-S may enjoy the same prestige and price premium that collectors bestowed upon the fabled Coombs Mk 2 Jaguar during the 1980s…

Best buys? This is always difficult when confronted with such a wide range of models, but off-the-cuff I would nominate: Most interesting 'enthusiast's car' – V12 manual (not dear, either). Most practical and cheap to run: 3.6 Coupe.

Best-handling and quickest: XJR-S 6.0-litre. Most sporting *and* practical (20mpg-plus): XJS 4.0-litre. Most individual: Cabriolet. Most eye-catching: red Convertible. Smoothest and most 'traditional Jaguar': low-mileage HE Coupe.

The inspection

Having defined character, we can move on to the nuts-and-bolts of choosing an XJ-S – or, if you already own one, help you assess what you have and maybe pinpoint areas which could be improved. Bear in mind, however, that an XJ-S is not usually a first-time buy, nor is it a beginner's car, so the following provides specific information on the XJ-S itself and is not a general used-car buyer's guide.

The length of this advice might seem to indicate that the XJ-S is nothing but a load of trouble, but rest assured that it has always been the most affordable, toughest and easiest and cheapest to maintain 150mph supercar ever made. If you want proof, try running an early 1980s Ferrari, Lamborghini or Aston Martin! So while the 'what to look for' list may be long, no car will suffer from all the faults described, while we are also talking about a great variety of models, some more than 20 years old.

Before you close in on the details, stand back and look at the subject car from a distance. XJSs tend to be driven fast, and therefore occasionally hit things hard, so look for poorly repaired accident damage. From the factory, door gaps, panel fit and shut lines were generally good, so be suspicious of any deviations. When sighted down the flanks and across the roof, no ripples should be present, and watch for different shades of paint on adjacent panels. Check the front inner wings and behind the boot carpeting for evidence of repairs.

All four wheels should be checked for visual alignment – even without incurring body damage, a badly 'kerbed' car can suffer a surprising degree of distortion in the rear wishbones or front suspension beam, the latter confirmed by observing the front mounting eyes – they should be parallel, but mis-alignment elsewhere tends to be amplifed at this point.

The bodyshell

Now the body can be examined more closely. On the subject of rust, Jaguar's anti-corrosion treatment improved steadily

Before closing in on the prospect, stand back and get an overall feel for the car and note any ripples or uneven gaps; no problems with this superbly original early car, though!

over the years, and the Venture Pressings-built shells (the revised rear-end cars from May 1991) were zinc-coated and wax-injected and are unlikely to show serious corrosion for many years.

Whilst XJSs have also proved to be less rust-prone than their saloon cousins, this does not mean that there are no 'terminal' examples around amongst earlier models, and the integrity of the bodyshell is a vital factor in (especially) pre-HE and early HE cars.

The first port of call should be the rear jacking point/radius-arm mounting area, including the chassis legs as they climb above the rear suspension 'cage'. Unless there is a very good reason not to, reject any car with extensive problems in this area. Whilst underneath, check the boot floor, sill lower seams, front jacking points and sill end closing panels. Strangely, unlike the saloons, the radiator support crossmember rarely rots.

Inside the car, check the inner sills where they meet the floor, particularly at the extreme ends. While the carpets are up, inspect the condition of the floor itself; again, the ends where it meets the vertical seat-pan and toe-board are particular problem areas.

The final 'terminal rejection area' is where the front wing top mounting flange meets the inner wing – a box-section runs along here, which can disintegrate and also affect the outer wing (a line of bubbles adjacent to the bonnet is the external telltale); in extreme cases the bulkhead and scuttle top panel are also affected.

If the car has survived so far, check the outer sills where they join the rear wings; a perfect seam should be seen, not a replica made from filler! A small magnet is useful for detecting this material on all outer panels, by the way. The rear lower quarter-panels are welded (not bolt-on, as on the saloons) and suffer both at their lower edge and the top seam where they meet the rear wings (hidden by the bumper). Also, look at the rear valance where it meets the boot floor, around the exhausts and the double-skinned area behind the rear bumper centre-section.

Before leaving the main bodyshell, three other areas should be observed: curiously, the inner face of the flying buttresses where they meet the boot aperture; the front wing to sill attachment point (the splash panels have to be removed to see this); and the front inner wings, just below the shock absorber

During the spring of 1991 the six-cylinder XJS lost its hyphen and gained the 4.0-litre engine, plus remodelled interior, side windows and rear end. *Photo: P Skilleter*

In 1995 Jaguar achieved its 60th year, marked in the range by the six-cylinder Celebration-model XJS coupe and convertible. Announced in May, the Celebration featured Aerosport cast-alloy wheels and distinctive interior trim changes. *Photo: Jaguar Cars*

top mounts. Problems can sometimes be found in isolation at these three places on otherwise rust-free cars, but the good news is that they are easily repairable.

The 'bolt-on' panels can be summarized thus:

Bonnet: Obvious rust is rare, but corrosion can take place between the inner and outer panels, reducing its strength; detect this by flexing the top corners when open – an internal crunching noise indicates trouble.

Bootlid: Most early bootlids will have some degree of rot to the lower skin – easily repairable if it hasn't spread to the inner frame. The separate hollow number-plate plinth is also a problem area.

Doors: Lower skin and inner panel front to rear, around the door mirror and the frame adjacent to the quarter-light all suffer.

Front wings: Check along the top fixing flange, attachment area to the sill and sometimes (strangely, on 1986–89 cars) above the headlamp.

Front lower valances: Just about everywhere!

If the foregoing puts you off, it should be stressed once more that we are talking of cars possibly over two decades old and that most of their contemporaries will have long since 'met their maker'. With patience, good, sound or easily repairable cars can be found.

Engine/mechanical

Mechanically, the XJS is very durable, but obviously all major components need assessment to avoid later expense (or to negotiate a better price!). A test drive should ideally be of 10 miles or more and take in traffic and the open road. The following should help identify any vices:

V12 engine

Whilst very strong and understressed, this all-aluminium power unit is easily damaged by neglect of the cooling system. Firstly, a high concentration of antifreeze should be present.

If this rule has been ignored, internal corrosion and subsequent head gasket failure can be expected.

Even worse, if the engine has been seriously overheated – for example if a perished hose or rotted header tank has burst, causing loss of coolant – the entire engine can 'banana'. The symptoms of this condition are decreased performance, lowered oil pressure, serious oil leaks (particularly from the rear main) and ultimately main bearing failure. A replacement engine is the only economic cure.

No Jaguar V12 is totally oil-tight, a reflection of the age of its design, although late engines are much better; slight seepage from most joints and seals, including the rear main, is therefore normal.

Actual oil consumption should be minimal, but even low-mileage engines can smoke from the exhaust for a brief period when starting from cold (due to oil running down the valve guides into the combustion chamber); this is acceptable so long as it clears after a few seconds.

All V12s should start promptly and immediately run on all 12 cylinders – this is surprisingly easy to detect and can be double-checked by feeling the smoothness of the gases exiting the exhaust pipes. Causes of misfiring or uneven running can be mechanical (lack of compression, burnt valves, etc), or stem from injection or ignition system maladies. (See the maintenance section for a fuller explanation.)

The engine should be mechanically quiet, but injectors and cams cause a lot of top-end 'tick'. Even on low-mileage (c 35,000 miles) engines the long duplex timing chain can be faintly audible – best described as a light tinkling noise from the front end at about 2,000rpm on the overrun. Should the tinkling develop into a more coarse, grating sound, attention is urgently needed as probably both chain and tensioner need replacing.

This should not be confused with other 'front-end' noises; the bearings in the alternator, water pump, fan drive, air conditioning compressor and belt idler tensioners can all be guilty. A 'whooshing' noise is an indication of a seized Torquatrol cooling fan drive, however, and this should be replaced before it launches itself through the radiator!

Oil should be fresh-smelling: dirty oil indicates poor servicing. Indicated oil pressure should be 60/75psi hot at approx

3,000rpm – it is normal for this to drop off to around 20psi at hot idle as long as it picks up instantly with revs. Remember that the most unreliable part of the lubrication system is the electric gauge sender itself, so if in doubt, double-check with a direct-reading instrument.

Six-cylinder engines
Despite having less cubic capacity to haul a similar (and substantial) weight around, it is difficult to fault the 3.6/4.0-litre AJ6/AJ16 engines, or pinpoint any recurring problems. Early engines were somewhat harsh, but this was soon cured. It is none the less wise to check for 'routine' engine faults – oil consumption, blue smoke, head gasket leakage and excessive or alarming mechanical noises. If present, such problems are likely to have been caused by neglect of coolant and oil levels rather than simply wear.

Ancillaries and belts should be checked as per the V12, but about the only problem endemic to the AJ6 was the poor 'drivability' commonplace on early manual cars; this was caused by overrun fuel cut-off due to ECU programming, which can be modified by specialists such as the appropriately named AJ6 Engineering.

Transmission
There are no special problems to be wary of. The Jaguar manual four-speed box occasionally fitted to early cars between 1976 and 1979 is an unburstable unit, although after high mileages the synchromesh can weaken and noise can develop in neutral due to countershaft bearing wear. However, parts availability for this box is good and repairs can be effected economically.

The 'six-cylinder' gearboxes, both auto and manual, are extremely reliable, but be warned that the Getrag five-speed is virtually a 'sealed for life' unit with low parts availability; so check carefully that all is well with it.

Clutches for both six and 12-cylinder cars are long-lasting, but if replacement is needed the job can be done without the trauma of engine removal required on previous manual Jaguars (although bellhousing bolts can occasionally seize).

The Borg-Warner Model 12 automatic fitted to the pre-1977 V12s was a reliable, though somewhat crude gearbox;

A crucial point is where the rear radius-arms mount to the body via rubber mountings.

Rust in the up-and-over chassis box-sections on which the rear subframe mounts means 'beware'. Try and judge the integrity of the bonded rubber mounts as well.

Bumper assembly and front valance have been removed here to show the crossmember which runs under the oil cooler. Usually it remains intact, but on some cars a replacement is necessary (and feasible).

Rust in the bonnet seams can be spotted visually, but flexing may reveal hidden rot aurally.

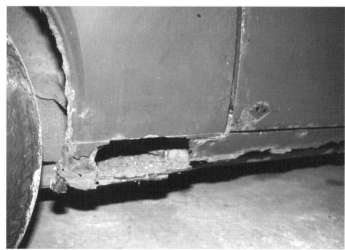

Rust in outer panels such as the sills and rear quarter-panel aft of the door should be self-evident – unless hidden by filler.

This car has stood in the open unused for many months, so the corrosion is excessive: but it serves to indicate danger points on the vertical bootlid panel.

Lower part of the front wing and the front valance are also vulnerable.

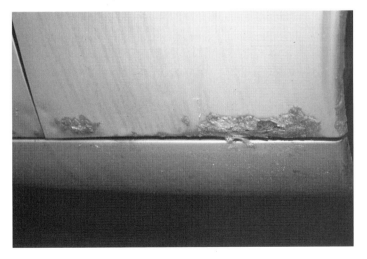

Examine the lower part of the front wing as it meets the sill, also the closing panels inside the wheelarch.

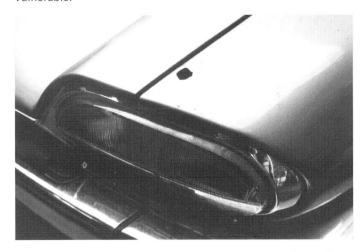

Strangely, some late 1980s cars seem prone to rust here, above the headlamp.

The V12 engine (this a near-perfect pre-HE car) may appear daunting – and it certainly can hit the pocket if it has not been maintained properly. Also check the cost of replacing all those hoses and vacuum pipes!

The correct percentage of anti-freeze is vital while, of course, loss of coolant will quickly ruin the engine. This can happen through a perforated header tank, so give it a look-over.

just check the fluid for evidence of slipping clutches. It should be clear red and almost odourless – dark browns and 'burnt nutty' smells mean trouble.

The replacement GM 400 (identifiable 'in car' by a large gap between P & R on the selector quadrant) was altogether smoother and more refined, but unfortunately less reliable. It was also programmed to be less sporty. Early GM boxes will not engage first whilst on the move (despite workshop manual tables stating the contrary), but by the introduction of the HE, revalving allowed first to be engaged by manual selector or kickdown – vastly improving drivability in traffic.

Fluid should be checked as per the Borg-Warner. Whining, whistling and whooshing noises are indicative of impending failure (front pump usually) when drive can be lost without further warning. Oil leaks attributed to the sump pan are usually, in fact, from the dipstick tube and modulator 'O' ring seals (easily repaired).

With all transmissions, a grinding noise on hard cornering is simply cured by replacement of the mount pin bush and realignment of the gearbox mounting crossmember.

The front of the engine is a mass of belt drives and ancillaries – this shows the big air conditioning compressor.

This is a Getrag gearbox being removed from a 3.6; spares are almost non-existant and an exchange or secondhand unit is usually the only answer in the unlikely event of failure.

The Salisbury limited-slip differential (LSD) is very reliable in all applications; some very slight noise can be expected, but it should not be excessive. The function of the LSD can be checked by jacking up one rear wheel and attempting to turn it (handbrake off and other wheels chocked!). If this is almost impossible, the Powr-Lok clutches are OK. Oil leaks are common (caused by the inboard brakes 'cooking' the seals), but these can be cured *in situ*.

Beware the Dana differential fitted spasmodically during approximately 1985–88. As with the Getrag gearbox, spare parts are unobtainable. This unit can be identified by its flat bottom and the brake caliper mounting bolts screwing into the side of the diff casing – unlike the Salisbury, where the bolts thread outwards into lugs on the output shaft assembly.

Suspension

If you thought we had covered all the areas of corrosion, think again! Two major rust points are associated with the suspension: the pressed-steel front subframe (feel behind the spring towers), and the rear, hollow, radius-arms – these latter can rust so badly that they actually break!

Check the differential (this is a Salisbury with the propshaft removed) for oil leaks, which are especially annoying if they have contaminated the inboard rear brakes.

Check the tyres; a good, correctly rated matched set is indicative of a caring owner. Odd wear patterns will point the way to other suspension faults, although all hard-driven XJ-Ss tend to punish the centre-section of the rear tyres.

The car should sit 'squarely' – front springs are prone to breakage and rears to sagging with age. Damping should be positive and leakage from shock absorbers is unacceptable. Also note that the front anti-roll bar vertical link bushes are prone to failure.

In fact all rubber bushes and mounts are subject to deterioration, softening and separating with age. On older cars, check the four 'V' mounts locating the rear suspension cage – jack up the car from the rear and see if the suspension stays on the ground!

At the front-end, normal checks should be carried out on balljoints, wishbone bushes and wheel bearings. Note that to achieve this the car must be supported under the spring pan if wear is not to be masked by the loading of the road spring.

Rear-end steer is most commonly caused by worn lower rear hub-carrier parts – quite complex to repair and set up correctly. Also check for excessive play in the rear wheel bearings, universal joints, wishbone inner pivots and final-drive output bearings.

A hard-driven (eg thrashed) XJS can suffer from the final-drive unit moving within the suspension cage – but it is difficult to spot the splits around the top mounting bolts and loose inner wishbone pivot bearers.

Steering
Up to around 1988, the steering is a little woolly as standard, with a rubbery feel around the straight-ahead position – this can be improved by replacing the mounting bushes (see maintenance chapter). Although the system is basically vice-free, there are a few symptoms to be aware of. Stiffness and notchiness can be caused by upper column bearing failure, a pump fault, simple lack of fluid, or seized suspension balljoints and/or lower steering column joints. Free play is usually due to sheared rack mounts, or failed lower column pivot. Rack leakage from both piston and gaiters is common after a high mileage, also inspect hoses for chafing.

This radius-arm is well and truly rusted through.

Brakes

On all models, the brakes should be positive, impressive and pull the car up squarely. Dead-feeling or heavy brakes can be due to seized caliper pistons, incorrect pad material or servo problems (sometimes just the air filter or vacuum non-return valves). A pulsing pedal points to cracked or distorted ventilated front discs. Fluid leaks are common from the remote reservoir to mastercylinder link pipes.

The handbrake with its 'drop down' lever is capable of performing well when all is as it should be – don't be persuaded otherwise. The rear brakes can suffer with oil contamination emanating from the final-drive, as mentioned earlier (except of course on late cars, where the discs are outboard).

On cars from 1988-on equipped with ABS, observe that the warning light goes out after a few seconds – and check that someone hasn't removed the bulb! The ABS function can be checked by road test (but use the rear-view mirror first!).

General

By modern standards, early Convertibles display an astonishing degree of scuttle shake over uneven surfaces, but this is normal (!) and was cured by Jaguar in May 1992 with an underside cross-bracing. Specialists such as Harvey Bailey Engineering and Classic Spares can supply such a device for earlier cars.

The Coupes should be leak-free from the body seals, Cabriolets and Convertibles likewise; problems can arise, but are rectifiable with patience. Cabriolets suffer from faded hoods and opaque (plastic) rear windows, these defects responding to specialist attention.

Exhaust system condition is usually self-evident. Factory systems improved in specification over the years (better-grade stainless employed in some sections); cheap aftermarket mild

Tyre types, wear patterns and condition can tell a lot about a car. Watch for wheels out of true and check the alloy wheels for corrosion, pitting and rim damage – this is the Kent Alloys item used on pre-HE cars.

steel units tend to be very short-lived and the stainless steel systems may vary in fit and quality.

The condition of interior and exterior fittings will be obvious – sagged headlining, distorted door trims and damp carpets (blocked air conditioning drain tubes are often to blame here) are common on older cars. Rusted front and rear bumper beams can be found on all years of XJ-S, but only the HE has the imagination to suffer from rotting chrome bumper sections!

Failed gas support struts will probably have been noticed at an earlier stage in the inspection when the bonnet collapsed on your head. Door locks and handles can malfunction in a variety of ways, including from corrosion. The front spoiler and its undertray are prone to damage or loss and the head-

The usual checks for wear apply to the front suspension – bushing on the anti-roll bar link seem shot on this car. Look for detached or holed gaiters and check condition of the ventilated discs.

Wear or damage to the upholstery, headlining and trim panels will be self-evident. This pre-HE car has the rare optional velour upholstery.

lamps should be checked for cracked lenses and dull reflectors – they are expensive to replace. Noisy fuel pumps and leaky fuel tanks (the hidden bottom surface pinholes where it sits on a soundproofing pad) are worthy of note.

Test the operation and function of all ancillaries – wiper motors and the heating/air conditioning system are particularly expensive to rectify. Owners often claim to have removed the air conditioning drive belt 'for economy', yet in such cases, strangely, the compressor is usually found to be seized…

The XJ-S interior is pretty durable (this is an early HE); check operation of all switches, instruments and (especially) wipers and air conditioning – repairs can be tedious and expensive.

Only the HE seems to suffer rust on the plated bumper sections!

A test drive should be long enough to get the engine oil (not just the coolant) completely up to operating temperature. Assess the suspension on bends and over poor surfaces – progress should be exceptionally smooth, quiet and free from rear-end steering.

The vacuum-controlled heater valve is also susceptible to jamming, open or closed, but is rather easier and cheaper to replace.

No car can be expected to be faultless, so prior to purchasing or rejecting a given vehicle it is a good policy to check with your favoured XJS specialist in order to determine the 'value' of each defect, both in terms of parts (new or used) and likely labour charges. In this way a sensible decision can be reached – and remember that in excess of 115,000 XJSs have been made, so there are plenty to see!

CHAPTER 10

Modification and maintenance

How to enhance ownership satisfaction

Modifying for performance

The XJ-S has proved to be the most popular Jaguar ever for aftermarket alteration, even more so than the E-type. This is because the XJ-S reacts well to sensible changes, and good results can be achieved quite cheaply.

One point to make straight away is that while it may be too soon to view any XJ-S as a true collector's item, thought should be given before altering a good, original-condition, pre-HE car. Such examples are already extremely rare and should be valued simply because of this.

In general terms, before altering anything, ensure that the car is up to manufacturer's specification. For instance, lower springs and stiffer shock absorbers will not improve handling if the wishbone bushes are worn! With old or high-mileage cars, simply making sure that everything affecting the car's dynamic abilities are in perfect condition – bushes, rack mountings, subframe mountings, dampers, brakes, tyres and so on – will often transform the whole feel of the vehicle without departing by one nut or bolt from the original specification. And for most people, an XJ-S in top condition provides more than ample measures of performance, handling and braking.

In fact rash changes can all too easily spoil the very virtues which make the XJ-S the car it is, without adding any true benefits; since the late 1940s successive generations of Jaguar engineers have been the envy of the world's motor industry for the way they have blended superb refinement and ride qualities with great handling. Care needs to be taken before you disturb this exemplary compromise between potentially opposing factors.

That said, there are always those who value precision of control over the last word in ride comfort and refinement. This is a perfectly valid philosophy and Jaguar themselves recognized this when they launched the Sports-pack 3.6 XJ-S and then the more ambitious JaguarSport variants. In fact if you want to make changes, firstly consider these carefully engineered packages. Or, if the original parts are no longer available, emulate the specifications as closely as possible.

Not that there are no good alternatives; some of the better independent specialists have evolved their own chassis upgrades which work very well – and as original JaguarSport components become more scarce, these will be increasingly relied upon by enthusiasts.

For example, Harvey Bailey Engineering's carefully matched shock absorber and anti-roll bar kits for the XJ-S achieve an excellent ride/handling compromise while greatly reducing body roll. Lister Cars (which grew out of WP Automotive, founded in the 1960s) have immense experience in modifying the XJ-S and offer chassis mods which range from the mild to near-race. In Germany, Arden also offer both modest and extreme suspension and steering upgrades (carrying, uniquely, official Jaguar approval) while back in England, Classic Spares can advise on and supply many handling items which they themselves have proved in competition at surprisingly modest cost. And this is by no means an exhaustive list – see Appendix G for addresses and further companies in this field.

Although the less experienced owner is best advised to fit a well-proven suspension package, it is possible to 'pick and mix', especially if you are working to a tight budget. But do

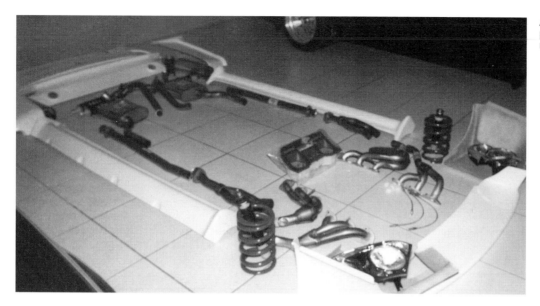

All the bits! Bolt-on body and suspension parts, plus V12 exhaust manifolds, from Paul Hands.

listen to the experts or, as already indicated, you might end up destroying the XJ-S's beautiful balance without making it any faster or more pleasant to drive.

While there is seemingly no upper limit on the possible scope and cost of modifications, for the more impecunious the most effective areas to tackle are:

Sports steering rack bushes: the best modification per pound available, these massively improve steering response and precision, but avoid solid bushes as these ruin refinement.

Smaller-diameter, thicker-rim steering wheel with, perhaps, a later quicker-ratio steering rack and/or JaguarSport power steering valve to complete the effect.

Sports front springs improve handling with surprisingly little effect on ride comfort.

Adjustable gas shock absorbers allow damping to be tuned to individual preference; Koni and Spax are favourites, the latter allowing simple 'on car' adjustment.

Rotation of rear radius-arm bushes through 90 degrees (voids run across car) improves rear-end location; specialized anti-tramp kits are also available.

Wheels and tyres can be updated to later specifications and beyond. But care is needed not to spoil the car's balance; ultra-low-profile tyres can make the ride very harsh. Follow specialist recommendations and avoid unknown and inappropriately rated makes of tyre.

Electric cooling fans can replace the Torquatrol units and reduce noise and petrol consumption.

The GM 400 transmission, with its American origins, can easily be uprated (by means of shift kits, modulators and torque converters) to any level from sportier response to full manual-only control.

Brakes are usually considered more than adequate, but harder semi-competition pads are available and recommended if you enjoy circuit driving days. Full lightweight competition brakes are available off-the-shelf, but the cost is awe-inspiring.

Engine modifications

These also can be taken to extremes, with very expensive large-capacity conversions available for both the V12 and straight-six engines; in addition, companies such as Lister,

Less compliant steering rack bushes dramatically improve steering precision, though the almost rock-solid type (top) are recommended only for racing – the modified bush (right) reduces rack movement compared with the standard item, left.

Arden and Chasseur offer supercharging or turbocharging. These conversions give the XJ-S staggering acceleration and top speed, but major work of this sort costs far more than most people pay for their complete car.

Frankly, no version of the XJ-S was underpowered and relatively few owners bother to seek extra horses, but if you do want a more spritely performance there is often no need to change the engine's internals. For instance, the simple deletion of the 'mid' silencers is worth around 25bhp on a V12 and gives a sportier exhaust note (replacement pipes are available to suit). A freeflow system is even better, but harder on the bank balance.

AJ6 Engineering are responsible for a wide range of developments for the AJ6 and V12 engines. Modified cylinder heads and large-capacity conversions are available, but performance

Firmer dampers give a more sporting feel to the XJ-S and Spax adjustables offer a convenient and affordable alternative to the standard items. Bilsteins are rated top by many, however.

Probably the ultimate for a roadgoing XJS: the 7.0-litre twin supercharged V12 by Lister Cars is for the wealthy only!

Affordable extra power for the V12 comes in the form of AJ6 Engineering's big-throttle conversion (indicated) and the high-flow air cleaners installed on this 1988 V12 Convertible.

Unlikely to be available indefinitely, both early and late-model Jaguar-Sport body kits look attractive. This early car was photographed at JaguarSport's original Kidlington facility.

US-style four-headlamp conversions are popular, especially as the round units are much less costly to replace.

can be optimized by remapped ECUs (electronic control units – the engine's brain), large and multiple-throttle conversions and high-torque inlet manifolds. Additionally, engines can benefit from AJ6 Engineering's enhanced-drivability ECUs – an economic way to improve throttle response.

Before leaving the subject of engines, remember that while extra power can be obtained quite easily, refinement may be lost. You can't always have your cake and eat it.

Interior and exterior upgrades

One benefit of the XJ-S's long production run is that an earlier car can be upgraded quite easily by fitting later components – from complete interiors to individual items such as steering racks, alternators, oil coolers, cooling systems and much more. Later automatic gearboxes can be fitted and manual transmission transplants are practical, too, pedal boxes and console tops being easily obtained from the 3.6.

Many of these parts can be found secondhand – at least in the UK – and thus quite cheaply, but if you are a beginner in

Comprehensive reshaping of the XJ-S is undertaken by Lister Cars, who also offer many other special parts.

Chasseur Developments make this subtle body kit for the XJS, as well as a twin turbocharger installation for the six-cylinder cars.

Hyper Engineering offer a range of affordable body styling items including new shape rear-light clusters, boot lid conversions and front and rear spoilers.

Early Convertibles benefit greatly from an anti-scuttle shake kit; this one is being fitted by Classic Engineering, of Waltham Cross.

such realms, do consult a genuine expert: some swops are by no means as straightforward as they may seem.

Body kits are about the most popular add-ons amongst XJ-S owners and many styles and qualities are available. Whatever the true aerodynamic advantages they bestow, they can certainly add individuality. At the time of writing (1996) both early and late JaguarSport body equipment is available from Jaguar dealers and the quality of components and fit is high. Other styles are available from specialists at varying prices and it is worth bearing in mind that fitting such equipment can often be cheaper than replacing a damaged bumper section with an original part.

The four-headlamp style is preferred by some, and for much the same cost as a pair of original elipsoidal units, the US export-type 5¾in lamps can be substituted. They are also much cheaper to replace if damaged, while their efficiency can be improved if four Cibie halogen dip/main units are employed.

For early Convertibles, anti-scuttle shake kits can be con-

Autostyle provide the XJ-S owner with a wide choice of custom parts, including this effective 'round dial' dashboard conversion for those who dislike the barrel-type instruments.

Still a favourite – the Motolita classic-style woodrim wheel has been popular since the 1950s and can look good against the XJS's own veneers.

sidered essential; they are relatively inexpensive and, after all, no Jaguar should be reminiscent of a Triumph Herald!

Beyond simple 'add on' styling kits, many more expensive options are possible. Four-seat conversions for the Cabriolet and Convertible turn them into family cars and, as mentioned in Chapter 8, Lynx (and Arden) produce estate variants, while wide-body and buttressless Coupe variants can be had; plus, of course, total reskins in completely different styles.

Even if you find your XJ-S bodyshell beyond hope, all is still not lost – DJ Sportscars produce the Dax Tojeiro, a fully developed Cobra lookalike utilizing all XJ-S mechanical components. Other Jaguar V12-based kit and component cars are also available. Conversely, in the United States there are a number of very professional home-grown V8 conversions to replace Jaguar engines which, for most Americans bereft of a ready supply of used replacement units, as in the UK, are difficult and expensive to rebuild.

Maintaining the XJ-S

It is not the purpose of this section to delve into restoration: that is not an economic proposition with the XJ-S anyway, and unless you enjoy the work for its own sake, your money is better spent on buying a sound, roadworthy car needing at most the sort of improvements which can go hand-in-hand with routine maintenance.

In general terms, the servicing, care and maintenance of an XJ-S is within the scope of the competent home mechanic. Even the electronic fuel injection, which made the average Jaguar club member of 1975 wonder how on earth such a car could be kept going by an enthusiast in 20 years' time, has now become commonplace – and can be maintained without the need for complicated equipment.

For those keen on retaining clean hands, franchised main dealer servicing is really only relevant to late cars or where a full service history is important. Below this, a network of

'Plus-2' conversions marketed by Classic Spares and several other companies can extend the useful life of an early Convertible for the family man.

Don't forget the official Jaguar range of accessories: this vacuum-formed tray protects the boot carpeting for those who habitually carry grubby objects or a lot of clutter.

independent Jaguar specialists exists, usually offering excellent knowledge of the cars and possessing special tools; their labour rates are about half those charged by main dealers. Some non-specialist garages and mobile mechanics charge around a third less again, but whilst perhaps adequate for run-of-the-mill servicing, their lack of specialist knowledge can sometimes lead to excessive costs due to 'repair by substitution' of some more complex systems.

Whoever undertakes the work, parts will be required. Even though for a prestige car Jaguar parts can be surprisingly inexpensive – less than for a lot of quite ordinary Japanese makes, for instance – main dealers should be used selectively by the owner of the older car: only some remain knowledgeable about long-obsolete models, while certain parts can be obtained more economically elsewhere. In real terms a number of items for the XJ-S are cheaper now than a few years ago, mainly service parts such as belts and filters.

The best parts sources for the older XJ-S are often, therefore, the independent Jaguar spares specialists. They can be found in the UK, Europe and the USA – seek recommendations from fellow Jaguar owners and the clubs. Such companies can usually supply new parts at discount prices and in some cases offer used items (even body panels) or reconditioned components such as water pumps, alternators, wiper motors, air conditioning compressors, steering racks, radiators and brake calipers, at a fraction of the cost new.

But it is false economy to use unbranded reproduction items in such areas as brake pads, discs, shock absorbers, suspension bushes and joints, tyres and exhaust systems. The XJ-S does not react well to these: their lower performance and higher wear rates detract from the very reasons for owning such a car in the first place.

As for body parts, with the exception of a few produced by Martin Robey and David Manners, there are no reproduction items; but thanks to the XJ-S's long and stable production run, interchangeability problems are few and new authentic Jaguar panels can be used on most cars.

Basic servicing information can be found in the 'High Street' workshop manuals while owners of pre-HE cars can obtain a reprint of the factory service manual (an early HE supplement is included). For later cars and all the six-cylinder variants, the only option to date is the expensive multi-volume work published by Jaguar themselves. In the writer's opinion, essential reading for those wishing to tackle the subject of fuelling is the excellent fuel injection manual published by AJ6 Engineering.

While full service and maintenance information is beyond the scope of this book the following pointers should help you obtain the best from your XJ-S:

A V12 imitating a V11 (or worse!) need not be too much of a problem assuming the compressions are good. Ensure that all the fuel injectors click audibly and sharply – if not, check

When replacing front suspension balljoints, fit XJ40-type sealed units (above) instead of the original complex kit (below), which doesn't last as long.

Shop around for your parts! Compared with a 1996 factory price of £550, an exchange wiper motor from Classic Spares costs under a third of that (top left). To cure front-end noises are a new fan belt tensioner, air conditioning idler with tensioner and V12 fan bearing housing assembly from the same company.

every electrical connector for corrosion and security. If this does not rectify matters, the injectors are probably gummed up (particularly common on cars that have been out of use for some time). To effect a cure, fill the fuel filter with neat injector cleaner, then spin the engine over to fill the injectors and leave them for some hours. If this fails, the injectors can be removed professionally and cleaned, then checked for a fraction of the replacement cost. Or the misfire could be ignition-related: the plugs and HT leads are prone to breaking down, but on OPUS-equipped cars (pre-HE) the Ferrite rods in the timing rotor beneath the rotor arm can fall out – replacement is the cure.

Underbonnet heat is the culprit behind many faults: poor performance is often due to perished or split vacuum pipes while the diaphragm in the distributor advance module also suffers. D Jetronic air pressure sensors have diaphragms which rupture, and they can suffer from multiplug connectors

Misfiring can often be traced to the electronically operated injectors.

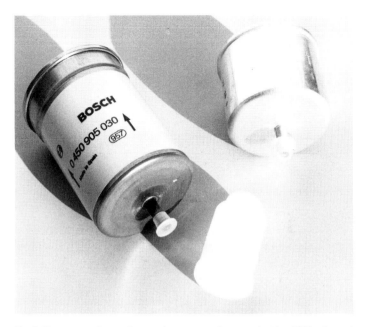

Fuel filters need regular replacement: largest is the HE's, found behind the spare wheel; smallest is the oft-forgotten one hidden under the battery; while the pre-HE filter has an underbonnet location on the offside front inlet manifold.

which have been fitted upside-down! Heat also degrades the cooling system hoses and drive belts: consider replacing them periodically to insure against overheating (use only genuine reinforced hoses). Note that the small-bore breather connections are prone to blockage – this can cause air locks.

Most heater and air conditioning faults tend to be complex and expensive, but before panicking, check the vacuum operated heater valve on the bulkhead: this can not only seize, but sometimes the operating lever can become internally detached, giving the external impression that it is still working!

Fuel pumps should run for a second or so when the ignition is switched on then shut down; investigate if it continues or risk a conflagration! Change the fuel filters regularly, not only the pressure filter, but also the nylon pick-up filter hidden in the tank below the battery; this could save the cost of a new pump.

The GM 400 transmission requires the filter in the sump to be changed regularly. Apparent oil leaks from the sump are usually from the modulator or dipstick tube 'O' ring seals – these should be 'helped' with additional silicone sealant.

The most common V12 engine oil leak is in the region of the oil filter head and can be cured with three 'O' rings and one gasket costing less than half a gallon of oil! At the front of the engine, the cause of a major oil leak can be as simple as the timing chain tensioner rubber access plug having fallen out.

Steering rack and pinion seal leakage can be rectified *in situ* at low cost (but not to the skin on your knuckles...).

Coat the lower steering column joints in grease to prevent the ingress of water and subsequent failure.

When replacing top and bottom front suspension balljoints,

A car for all seasons: both open and closed XJS variants made their last official appearance at a UK motor show in October 1995. Although it approached obsolescence in 1996, the XJS continues to hold great appeal for enthusiasts.

fit the latest-spec sealed XJ40-type units: they are easier to fit than kits and, despite the lack of grease nipples, seem to last around 70,000 miles.

Jaguar provide many front suspension adjustments (*eg* camber, castor and tracking); use them and you will be rewarded – ignore them and you will have the car you deserve!

Alloy wheel-to-hub mating surfaces should be lightly greased to prevent wheels seizing-on – awkward to rectify on a rainy motorway hard shoulder at night with your best suit on! Alloy wheels can be refurbished and even rim damage repaired much more cheaply than replacement.

The conscientious owner will pressure-wash the underside and treat the bodywork at least once a year with a good-quality rustproofing compound (such as Dinitrol, Waxoyl or Tectyl). See Chapter 9 for the rust danger spots, and in addition to the normal box-section treatments, remove the rubber bumper covers and treat the beams before replacing the covers. Also coat the underside of the HE's chrome bumper sections. Finally, inject the hollow rear suspension radius-arms.

If you are an owner, follow the advice above, learn the owner's manual by heart, read whatever workshop manuals you can obtain, and really come to know your car. That way you will be able to get the best from it, either by doing some or all of the necessary maintenance yourself, or by being able to assess the quality of work carried out by others.

The Jaguar XJ-S is a wonderful car; it is not without faults or idiosyncrasies and is undoubtedly large for essentially a two-seater, but for a blend of performance, lithe grace and mechanical toughness it outshines most other luxury sports-tourers. It will surely continue to give pleasure to many thousands of owners for many years yet.

APPENDIX A

Technical specifications

V12 MODELS

XJ-S GT Coupe, September 1975. Length 15ft 11½in; width 4ft 1½in; height 4ft 1½in; wheelbase 8ft 6in; track (front) 4ft 10in; track (rear) 4ft 10½in; weight 33½cwt (3,710lb); suspension (front) subframe-mounted double wishbones/coil springs, telescopic dampers, anti-roll bar; suspension (rear) subframe-mounted driveshafts/lower forks/trailing arms, twin telescopic damper/coil spring units per side, anti-roll bar. Engine: 60deg V12 all-alloy, single ohc per bank, bore and stroke 90 x 70mm, 5,343cc (326cu in), fuel injection; 285bhp at 5,500rpm, 294lb ft at 3,500rpm (244/269 US-spec). Transmission: three-speed automatic to Salisbury Powr-Lok final-drive, 3.07:1 ratio (3.31 optional), or four-speed all-synchromesh manual (1976–79).

HE, July 1981. As GT Coupe except: 5.3-litre May-head engine giving 295bhp at 5,000rpm with 12.5:1 CR, 2.88 final-drive; leather and veneer interior, domed alloy wheels and restyled bumpers incorporating indicator lights front and foglamps rear. January 1982: S3-style bumpers. October 1983: headlamp wipe/wash, trip computer, digital-tuning stereo radio/cassette, cruise control all standard (13334).

V12 HE Cabriolet, July 1985. Basic specification as for HE Coupe except: Weight 35cwt (3,920lb). Performance: 0–60mph 7.7sec, 0–100mph 18.7sec, maximum speed 140mph. Fuel consumption 13–17.5mpg.

Revised XJS V12 5.3, May 1991. As for HE except: black grille, Venture Pressings-built, zinc-coated bodyshell with flared sills, extended side glass area and new rear-end with rectagular lights; revised interior including round dials replacing barrel minor instruments, new sports seats, redesigned rear seats, upgraded audio equipment; 5.3-litre engine now with Lucas 26 CU fuel control system, revised fuel rail and injectors, new inlet manifold casting carrying 'Jaguar V12' logo; bhp now 280, Touring suspension standard, Sports optional. May 1992: tubular front underbody bracing introduced on Convertible and optional airbag offered.

Revised V12 6.0-litre XJS Coupe and Convertible, May 1993. As previous model except: engine now 90 x 78.5mm, 5,994cc with new forged steel crankshaft replacing cast-iron type, revised combustion chambers and camshaft profiles, new cylinder liners and lower (11:1) CR; 308bhp at 5,350rpm, 355lb ft torque at 2,850rpm. New four-speed GM4L80-E automatic gearbox with Sport/Normal modes, new torque converter with lock-up clutch. Sports suspension (Bilstein dampers) standard on Coupe, optional on Convertible, 7 x 16in five-spoke alloy wheels (forged lattice optional), outboard rear brakes, ZF steering rack. New heating/air conditioning and security systems. Convertible now 2-plus-2 (two-seater available to special order). Front and rear moulded, colour-keyed bumpers on all models.

XJR-S MODELS

XJR-S 5.3, 1988 (including 100 Le Mans special editions in Tungsten Grey). Basic specification as for 5.3 Coupe except: uprated suspension and steering, 15in Speedline alloy wheels and body kit. August 1989: uprated suspension and steering, 16in Speedline alloy wheels, new body kit and JaguarSport-developed, 78.5mm stroke, 5,993cc, Zytek engine management unit giving 318bhp. XJR-S discontinued after production 6.0 XJS was announced in May 1993. Note: 50 XJR-S Coupes and 50 XJR-S Convertibles were built for the US market.

SIX-CYLINDER MODELS

XJ-S 3.6 Coupe, October 1983. Basic specification as for V12 except: weight 32cwt (3,584lb). Engine: all-alloy straight-six, bore and stroke 91 x 92mm, 3,590cc (219cu in), fuel injection, twin ohc, four valves per cylinder; 225bhp at 5,300rpm, 240lb ft at 4,000rpm. Transmission: Getrag five-speed manual (overdrive fifth gear) to Salisbury Powr-Lok final-drive, 3.54:1 ratio. January 1986: herringbone tweed cloth centre-section to seats. February 1987: engine refinement changes and microfuelling, plus four-speed ZF 4HP 22 automatic gearbox optional. September 1987: Sports handling pack introduced as standard with stiffer springs and firmer damping, reduced power assistance, firmer rack mountings, no-cost optional wider Pirelli P600 235/60 tyres.

XJ-SC 3.6 Cabriolet, October 1983. Engine/chassis as per 3.6 Coupe except: weight 32½cwt (3,640lb), height 4ft 2in. January 1986: herringbone tweed cloth centre section to seats. February 1987: engine refinement changes and microfuelling, plus four-speed ZF 4HP 22 automatic gearbox optional.

Revised **XJS 4.0 Coupe**, May 1991. Basic data as for 3.6 except: AJ6 engine now longer-stroke, catalyst, 91 x 102mm, 3,980cc unit giving

223bhp at 4,750rpm; twin mass flywheel; gearbox either new ZF 4HP24 four-speed auto or Getrag 290 three-plane five-speed manual. Body now Venture Pressings-built, zinc-coated shell with flared sills, black grille, extended side glass area and new rear-end with rectangular lights; revised interior including round dials replacing barrel minor instruments, new sports seats, redesigned rear seats and upgraded audio equipment; Sports suspension standard.

XJS 4.0 Convertible, May 1992. Basic data as for 4.0 Coupe except: fitted with tubular front underbody bracing; optional airbag.

XJS 4.0 Coupe and Convertible, June 1994. Fitted with AJ16 engine June 1994 with improved induction, GEMS engine management and on-board diagnosis, sequential fuel injection, low-loss catalyst; 244bhp at 4,700rpm. Plus low-inertia torque converter, redesigned interior, 'sculptured cloth' (leather optional) trim with Coupe-style rear seats in Convertible, five-spoke alloy wheels and colour-keyed radiator grille, headlight surrounds and door mirrors.

'Celebration' 4.0 Coupe and Convertible, from May 1995. Basic specification as before except: Aerosport cast alloy wheels, black front grille, chrome door mirrors, twin coachlines.

APPENDIX B

Location of numbers and vehicle identification

Note: When purchasing a vehicle it is advisable to compare the vehicle (chassis) number and the numbers of major components on the documentation against those on the car and its components. The following will help you to find these numbers and interpret them.

Location of numbers
Engine:
V12 – stamped on top surface of bellhousing mating flange central to 'Vee'.
AJ6 – stamped on flange adjacent to power steering pump housing.

Chassis number:
Pre-Vehicle Identification Number system (up to May 1978) – stamped on right-hand inner wing strut support bracket.
VIN (introduced May 1978) – stamped on bulkhead strut support panel. Note: Early replacement bodyshells display no numbers at all. In recent years the factory have supplied shells – appropriately stamped – only when proof of destruction of original shell has been provided.

Body number:
Riveted plate on rear panel behind bumper.

Gearbox:
BW 12 and GM 400 automatic – on manufacturer's riveted-on I/D plate on left-hand side.
Four-speed manual – on horizontal surface of aluminium top cover and vertical left-hand rear lug on cast-iron casing.

Car identification (chassis) plates
Pre-VIN cars – oblong aluminium plate stating 'Jaguar Cars BL UK Ltd' riveted onto left-hand inner wing top surface between strut support bracket and bulkhead. Stamped with car (chassis) number and engine, body and gearbox numbers.

VIN cars: square aluminium plate, now stating 'British Leyland UK Ltd', in same location stamped with VIN plus paint and trim codes. 'Jaguar Cars Ltd' substituted some time after the company's privatization in 1984.

In approximately 1987, the metal chassis plate was deleted in favour of 'self destruct' sticker located in left-hand door shut B-post or above left-hand headlamp pod, carrying 'Jaguar Cars Ltd', VIN and trim and paint codes.

Vehicle Identification Number (VIN) interpretation
To unify vehicle identification worldwide, legislation required the use of Vehicle Identification Numbers (VIN) by October 1, 1979 and these were adopted by Jaguar in May 1978. They comprise a sequence of letters and numbers identifying the manufacturer, model, specification, emission equipment etc. They are followed by the individual car number.

The first three letters denote manufacturer, SAJ for Jaguar; the fourth letter denotes marque – J = Jaguar, D = Daimler; the fifth letter denotes models – N = XJ-S, S = XJR-S, T = XJ-S special edition; the sixth letter denotes class of vehicle – A = baseline, J = Japan, K = Japan with airbag, L = Canada, M = Canada with airbag, V = USA-spec with manual belts, W = USA-spec with driver airbag, Y = USA-spec with passive belts; the seventh letter denotes body variant – C = Cabriolet, D = Convertible, E = Coupe, F = 2+2 Convertible; the eighth letter denotes engine type (see below); the ninth figure is a number indicating transmission and steering – 3 = auto RHD, 4 = auto LHD, 7 = manual RHD, 8 = manual LHD; the 10th letter denotes model or year change – A = XJ-S original-spec, B = HE Coupe, C = AJ6 Coupe and Convertible, D = V12 Convertible, E = facelift – 1992 model-year except USA, Canada and Korea, where from 1981 the letter indicates year of build (1981 = B, and so on); the 11th letter indicates emission control equipment (see below); finally, figures 12–17 are the vehicle's unique number, commencing with 100001.

Engine and emission control equipment can be identified as below. Engine type is denoted by prefix letter eight:

B = 3.6 4VB

C = 3.6 4VC or 3.6 4Y (post ECS)
D = 3.6 4VD or 4.0 4Y
E = 3.6 4VE
K = 5.3   F
S = 6.0
V = 5.3   A
W = 5.3   B or 5.3 (post ECS)
X = 5.3   C
Y = 5.3   D
Z = 5.3   E

Prefix letter 11 denotes a wide variety of emission specifications for different markets, too numerous to list here; or, the manufacturing plant (Browns Lane) is indicated by 'C' for all markets up to the 1987 model-year. Contact your dealer if further clarification is sought.

APPENDIX C

Launch dates and initial prices

Note: Dates are those pertaining to the UK market. Some models were launched at slightly later dates in the US and other markets. Introductory and discontinuation VINs are given where known (some 'introductory' numbers predate announcement dates and indicate production prototypes).

1975 XJ-S GT Coupe V12 5.3 announced September (£8,900); 2W 1001, 2W 50001

1981 XJ-S HE Coupe V12 5.3 announced July (£18,950); 105048

1983 XJ-S 3.6 Coupe announced October (£19,248); 112586
XJ-SC 3.6 Cabriolet announced October (£20,756); 112588

1985 XJ-SC HE V12 Cabriolet announced July (£26,995); 125021

1986 XJ-S Convertible V12 (Hess & Eisenhardt) announced November ($47,000)

1987 XJ-S 3.6 Coupe Sportspack announced September (£23,500); 139052. 3.6 Cabriolet discontinued; 148594

1988 V12 Cabriolet discontinued February; 148594
V12 Convertible announced April 1988 (£36,000); 147269
XJR-S 5.3 Coupe (including Le Mans special edition) announced August (£35,000)

1989 XJ-S Collection Rouge announced June (US$51,000)
XJR-S Coupe 6.0 announced August (£45,000)

1990 XJ-S 5.3 Coupe Le Mans special edition announced September (£38,700)

1991 New XJS range (restyled rear-end, 4.0 engine) introduced May: 4.0 Coupe (£33,400), V12 5.3 Coupe (£43,500), V12 5.3 Convertible (£50,600); 179737. Revised XJR-S announced September

1992 XJS 4.0 Convertible (£39,00) announced May; 184574

1993 Revised (moulded-bumper) XJS range announced May: XJS V12 6.0 Coupe (£45,100), 6.0 2-plus-2 Convertible (£52,900), 4.0 Coupe (£33,600) and 4.0 2-plus-2 Convertible (£41,400); 188105. 1994 model year range announced September; 190528

1994 AJ16 engine fitted to 4.0 models from June: (4.0 Coupe (£36,800), 4.0 Convertible (£45,100), V12 Coupe (£50,500), V12 Convertible (£58,800)

1995 'Celebration' 4.0 Coupe (£38,950) and 4.0 Convertible (£45,950) models announced May. V12 models ceased regular production *circa* July
Final price 1996 model-year 4.0 Convertible North America $61,570

Production changes by date, chassis and engine number

The following information on major (and some minor) specification changes has been obtained from various sources, but many anomalies arise, particularly in the early years. Jaguar were a relatively small company and tended to use parts as and when they were available, while for various reasons individual cars (or small batches) could be produced out of chassis number sequence. Also, many cars have been modified retrospectively.

Through its 21-year lifespan the pace of development accelerated exponentially – from a slow start between introduction and the HE, the early Eighties brought a multiplicity of body styles and engine variants. The late Eighties continued the theme with international leglislation playing its part. The Nineties heralded changes every few months – including the car's only major facelift despite a production run longer than that of the legendary E-type.

Production changes – pre-HE

Sept 75
2W1001 RHD/2W50001 LHD
      XJ-S introduced.
2W1191/51038
      Rear calipers modified, pistons and dust boots now same pattern as front calipers.

Feb 76
2W1199/51091
      Door trim attachment improved.
2W1211   Modified throttle pedal assembly – strengthened with improved grip.
2W1258/51213
      XJ-S boot strip modified with finer lettering replacing saloon type.
2W1649/51882
      Oil gauge and sender revised – can be identified by offset terminal on sender replacing central type.
2W1695/51947
      Metric threads replaced BA on scuttle vent grille attachment.
2W1718/51947
      Revised door aperture trim replaced early pattern – chrome end finishers deleted.
2W1814/52074
      3-bolt pulley PAS pump replaced single-bolt.
2W1899/52197
      Bonnet gas strut attachment modified with bolts replacing countersunk screws.
854551   Cannister type oil cleaner assembly replaced element type. Top of transmission tunnel aperture increased in size (auto and manual top covers modified to suit).

Oct 76
2W2030/52556
855203   Revised EFI – power amplifier, pressure sensor, cold-start injectors, thermo timeswitch and distributor.
2W2061/52527
      Revised position of front brake pipes.
2W2149   Lucas 25ACR (66AMP) alternator replaced 20ACR Motorola.
2W2177/52788
      Revised brake servo (vacuum take-off position).
856454   Modified oil pump.
2W2541/53172
      Revised exhaust system – shorter downpipes, altered inter-pipes, mid-boxes and over-axle pipes with 3-bolt flange fittings.
2W2574/53170
      Front stub-axles enlarged to minimize pad knock-off from flexing; uprights, steering arms and wheel bearings modified to suit metric caliper bolts.
2W2780/50203
      Steering wheel adjuster altered.

Apr 77
2W2833/57507
857017   GM 400 auto transmission introduced – revised drive, plate torque converter mountings, damped propshaft, revised selector mechanism, cylinder block (dowel lugs position), crankshaft (location flange for torque converter).
2W3044/53640
      Manual transmission cars: 'triangular' brake and clutch pedals replaced by square saloon types.

Nov 77
858632   Stronger manual transmission selector shafts.

Feb 78
2W4023/54660

1978 model-year modifications introduced.
All-chrome radiator grille replaced black infill. Body colour replaced satin black number-plate panel, silver grey replaced satin black on rear lamp infills. Polished stainless steel B-post trims replaced by satin black. Revised front seat slides and mountings. Large towing eyes fitted to front and rear suspension. Wheel nuts ⅞" instead of ¾" AF.

Note: In reality these visual changes were introduced 'piecemeal' – many earlier cars have body-colour number-plate panel and chrome radiator grille.

2W4668/55507

Upper steering column and mountings revised.

2W4731/55690

Handbrake calipers revised.

May 78 VIN Numbering system introduced.
8510195 Air filter boxes modified to combat covers 'blowing off' under spitback conditions – lower mounting flange has positive toothed location.

Oct 78
8511262 Opus ignition amplifier relocated to front crossmember.
101814 Last official production factory 'manual' car.
8513094 Single 'V' water pump pulley replaced twin 'V'.

Jan 79
101179 Dual-calibrated mph/kph speedo (at last for a GT!).
101801 Revised exhaust downpipes, 2-bolt flanges replaced 4-bolt.
8513094

Apr 79
101855 home/101878 export

1979 model-year modifications
Large square-type remote mirrors replaced bullet type. Trim-colour centre console replaced black – contrasting-colour S3 XJ saloon-type carpets. Offside-mounted remote aerial replaced nearside location (export 104667). Screw-in electric cooling fan sensor replaced push-fit in waterpump elbow.

Note: Some elements of the 1979 MY package appear earlier – particularly the revised mirrors.

Jan 80
103476 Rear foglamps fitted below rear bumper, UK/Europe cars.

Nov 80
104146 Digital P Jetronic injection system introduced – visually
8516401 indentified by single round-section fuel rail replacing previous twin.

10:1 compression ratio, modified inlet and exhaust valves, revised auxiliary air system.
4-bolt Torquatrol fan drive with plastic fan replaced single-bolt/steel fan-type; cooling atmospheric expansion bottle fitted under nearside front wing. Fuel filter relocated to boot, revised fuel pump and mountings. Chassis to engine mounting brackets strengthened.

104373 Metric PAS pump replaced imperial (with associated pipework).
8517194 Sump drain plug position moved from side to rear of pan (allows draining without removing ancillaries).
104667 Flush-fit remote offside aerial introduced.

Note, pre-HE models: During the production run, many variations of emission control and lighting etc were available to suit export legislation. Overrun valves (fitted to front of inlet manifolds) were fitted to all manuals, some early automatics, all digital cars and some export market cars.

Jul 81
105048, Eng No 8518001 HE introduced.
Revised engine with 'May Fireball' heads; P Jetronic fuel injection carried over from digital pre-HE; Lucas constant-energy ignition system replaced OPUS; revised cooling system with improved bleeding (anti-airlock) and atmospheric expansion tank; 2.88 diff replaced 3.07; Lucas A133 75amp alternator replaced 25 ACR Motorola 66amp; 6½" starfish alloy wheels replaced 6" GKN sports type. 215/70 x 15 (Dunlop D7/ Pirelli P5) tyres replaced 205/70 x 15 (Dunlop D1). Exhaust tail trims 'belled' instead of 'turned in'. Plastic multi-blade cooling fan and 4-bolt Torquatrol unit replaced steel single-bolt version.

Revised switchgear and graphics; key-operated central locking replaced console switch-activated type; revised wiper operation incorporating delay wipe; electric door mirrors replaced manual control; delay added to courtesy lamps, red door guard lamps fitted to rear of pockets, microswitch-operated boot illumination added.

Upgraded interior, all-leather trim, elm veneer infills on dash and door cappings. Revised-pattern steering wheel (as S3 saloon). Oatmeal carpet boot trim replaced black. Door seals revised from lip-type to tubular-section (improved sealing and wind noise control).

Revised-pattern headlamps, single H4 bulb replaced twin biode body piping added between front wings and scuttle panel; side repeaters fitted to front wings; bumpers now non-impact absorbing (home market) with chrome top trims; foglamps fitted in rear bumper beam; antique-style bonnet badge and broad double coachlines added. Antique-style Jaguar badge replaced silver plastic between reversing lamps; revised (XJS HE) boot badging.

Changes by VIN number
105381 Black infill outer door handles introduced.

106259	Revised heater motor assembly (plastic fan replaced steel).
106452	Rear anti-roll bar deleted (revised radius-arms).
107139	Revised boot trim – soft black vinyl spare wheel cover replaced one-piece moulded wheel/battery cover.
107197	Chrome infill replaced silver grey on rear lamps.
(109030 USA/Canada)	
107865	Metric PAS rack introduced and revised track rod ends (can be identified by reduced-diameter threads on track rod).
107929	Black infill interior door handles replaced all-chrome types.
107982	Deletion of PWDA (brake pressure warning differential activator) switch – revised front brake pipes, now 'green'-coated anti-corrosion.
108321	Cruise control modified, ECU revised, diff/propshaft-mounted sensor deleted in favour of transducer signal from gearbox.
109239	Brake servo vacuum valves revised.
109447	Over-axle exhaust mountings modified – no longer handed.
110191	Screen washer reservoir and pump enlarged.

Oct 83

| 112253 | 3.6 Coupe introduced. |
| 112314 | 3.6 Cabriolet introduced. |

AJ6 cast-crank engine, 5-speed manual Getrag gearbox, 3.54:1 diff ratio, reversed-pinion steering rack with stiffer torsion bar (2.75 turns).
Revised spring/anti-roll bar rates (no rear bar).
Lucas P digital injection and constant engine ignition.
Revised badging including antique 'S' motif (replacing V12) on radiator grille.

1984 MY	Body-in-white changes – increased size of gearbox access plates. Handbrake access hole now circular (formerly square). Brackets for early energy absorbing bumpers deleted from lower rear quarters. Hard plastic spoiler replaced rubber type. Standard equipment (V12), optional 3.6: headlamp wash/wipe (with enlarged twin-pump reservoir) and modified headlamp trims; trip computer (replacing analogue clock); cruise control, improved ICE.
113537	Electric speedometer and gearbox-mounted transducer introduced across range.
123281	Hirshmann one-piece aerial replaced remote motor type (offside) – revised boot trim to suit.

1985 MY
Jul 85

| 125020 | V12 Cabriolet introduced. |

V12 motif replaced HE on bootlid; walnut burr replaced elm on interior wood trim (V12 only). Doeskin sunvisors and A-post trims replaced black. Chrome seat adjuster bar replaced black. Cloth seat option introduced. Metric door lock assembly. Dana diff optional – identified by flat lower surface and caliper bolts threading into diff casing.

127026	V12 ignition amplifier spec change.
128811	3.6 balancing tolerances improved – a mass of modifications introduced piecemeal since introduction in order to improve engine refinement.
126321	V12: modified transmission oil cooler pipework – increased diameter.

1986 MY

| 130952 | Computer air conditioning introduced – identifiable by MAN/AUTO push-pull function to LH rotary switch. |
| 134282 | 3-point rear interia belts introduced (shelf-mounted reel). |

1987 MY
Sept 87

139052	3.6 Sportspack option, 235/60 x 15 Pirelli P600 tyres on 6½ x 15 lattice alloy wheels. Lock fitted to rack decreasing lock to lock from 2.75 to 2.5 turns – increasing turning circle from 12m to 13.1m; modified rack bushes, revised spring, anti-roll bar and damper rates. Rear anti-roll bar re-introduced.
1309522	'Computer' air conditioning introduced – identifiable by manual/automatic push-pull function on LH rotary switch.
134282	Three-point rear inertial belts introduced (shelf-mounted reel).
108285	3.6 engine: Bosch DW 1.7k 'gear reduction' starter motor replaced Lucas pre-engaged M45.

Feb 87, '1987½ MY'

3.6: four-speed 4HP22 automatic option and micro-fuelling integrated engine management system introduced. Further refinement modifications: 'XJ40' round air filter replaces V12 panel type. V12: 16CV ECV replaces 6CV.
Revised centre console and radio surround, 'ski slope' now wood-veneered (replacing black vinyl); revised switchgear. Heated door mirrors and washer jets (dual jets replace single central twin). Stainless steel sill treadplates replace grey plastic. Revised sculptured steering wheel. On coupe, locking filler flap replaces locking cap. Shaped 'sports' seats with modified floor mountings – seat-belt buckle mounted on seat frame.
Hella 'computer' cruise replaces AE Econocruise control. Voltage indicator deleted in favour of conventional ignition warning lamp. V12 (6-cylinder optional): front foglamps, electric lumbar support and seat heating.

| 1099970 3.6 engine | Bosch 90amp alternator replaces 75amp Lucas A133, water pump (shallower impellor.) 'Polyvee' drivebelt replaced 'V'-belt with revised damper and pulleys. |

Sept 87

139052   3.6 'Sportspack' option introduced. 235/60 x 15 Pirelli P600 tyres on 6½ x 15 lattice alloy wheels (replacing 6 x 15 'Pepperpot' wheels). Lockstops fitted to rack decreasing 'lock to lock' from 2.75 to 2.5 turns – increasing turning circle from 12m to 13.1m. Modified rack bushes. Revised spring, damper and anti-roll bar rates, rear anti-roll bar reintroduced.

144700   (V12 8S57572) Modified waterpump, countersink bottom fixing bolt to clear modified crank damper. Polyvee beltdrive replaces single 'V'. Bosch 115amp alternator replaces Lucas 75amp A133.
(3.6 141910) Bosch 115amp alternator replaces Bosch 90amp.

146955   Lucas 73351 fuel pump replaces 73175 type (interchangeable).

March 88, '1988½ MY'

147269   Teves ABS introduced. Revised front suspension vertical links, rear hub carriers and hubs to accommodate sensors. Washer bottle moved to under OSF wing, (V12: air filters moved forward). Sportspack lattice alloys and P600 tyres standardized across range, XJ40-type sealed suspension balljoints introduced. Minor fuse repositioning. (V12: Lucas M80 'R' gear reduction starter motor replaces M45 pre-engaged) 'optionally' introduced. V12 convertible introduced.

148782   Keikert central locking system replaces Lucas – now activates bootlid lock. Revised relays and ECU.
Bonnet insulation, coachlines and ICE revised. Instrument panel printed circuit modified.

Nov 88, 1989 MY

       157118 V12 coupe
       156989 V12 convertible
       157116 2.6 coupe
       Marelli digital ignition introduced on V12. Can be identified by 'lump' on passenger sidepost kickpanel to accommodate ECU. Modified cylinder block, crankshaft, damper and air cleaners to accommodate sensors (allows V12 to run on 95 or 91octane unleaded fuel). Sportspack available on V12 coupe. GM400 transmission recalibrated for improved responsiveness.

March 89   3.6 now adapted to run on unleaded 95 octane fuel (kit JLM1825 available to convert all 'microfuelled' cars).

Aug 89, 1990 MY

165790   Electrolux 'linkage drive' wiper system replaced Lucas rack type – park side position reversed, spoke tilt-action steering wheel (replaced fore-and-aft adjustment), redesigned stalk controls; ignition switch moved from facia to steering column (Ford-type airbag standard on US-market cars: self-contained unit – no external sensors). Catalyst optional on home-market cars. Steering rack standardized with 3.6 (pinion hydraulic connections facing forward with modified pipework). Trim colour dashboard surround replaced black, hinge-down underpanels to improve fuse/relay access; revised outer door handles with 'softer' profile.
Cruise-control recall on 1982–1990 model cars due to possible malfunctioning valve actuators (cruise may fail to disengage): extra vacuum dump-valve fitted to OSF inlet manifold.

Sept 90

176103   Catalyst converters now standard on UK market.

Oct 90   Fuel tank recall due possible leakage caused by excessive pressurization; cars updated to new specification fuel tanks (identified by solid pipe exiting from tank towards fuel pump – replaced flexible hose with union).

Nov 90   All XJS panels now supplied by Venture Pressings.

May 91

179737   Revised XJS range introduced: 4.0 replaces 3.6 litre, major re-engineering of bodyshell (180 new panels), revised neutral density rear lamp clusters, radiator grilles reverts to 1975-style black; bonnet panel commonized with V12. Interior upgrade included round-dial minor instruments. Switchable ZF4HP22 automatic box replaced by ZF4HP24 type, Getrag 290 three-plane gearbox replaced five-plane 256. V12: 26CV fuel control system replaced 16CU (incorporated diagnostic facility); revised fuel rail and injectors.

Sept 91   Revised XJR-S 6.0-litre with new, more integrated body-styling kit on latest bodyshell, 333bhp engine with catalyst standard.

Feb 92   Recall on Marelli ignition V12 cars (1989–91) due to HT lead possibly making contact with PI hose.

Feb 92

184574   4.0 convertible introduced.

May 93

188105   Revised 'moulded bumper' range introduced.

Sept 94

190528   1994 model year range introduced.

June 94   AJ16 engine replaced AJ6 in six-cylinder models.

Changes by engine number

(V12)
8S24175 Metric-threaded cylinder heads, cam carriers and water rails introduced (engine previously 'all imperial').
8S26992 Piston spec modified.
8S27297 Inlet manifolds modified (drillings for cold-start injectors deleted).
8S31737 Modified drive plate.

1986
8S41339 Spark plug spec changed. NGK BR7EFS replaced B6EFS.
8S41344 Sump oil baffle plate and windage tray modified.
8544227 Water pump bearing size increased.
8544317 Full-flow oil cooling replaced previous relief-flow system.
(8542379 Germany) Revised cooler/pipework and oil cleaner head, relief valve higher-rated. Pick-up pipe (in sump) increased in diameter. Lower front grille modified to clear cooler.
8545527 GM 400 transmission revalved, modified sump pan.

APPENDIX E

XJ-S annual production and Jaguar milestones

1975 – 1,245 – Launch year; Jaguar board abolished under BL; oil crisis hits sales of thirsty cars; Group 44 win SCCA Production Championship with V12 E-type in the USA
1976 – 3,082
1977 – 3,890
1978 – 3,121 – Jaguar now operates within Jaguar Rover Triumph (JRT); Group 44 win SCCA TransAm Championship with XJ-S
1979 – 2,405 – Series 3 saloon launched; JRT disbanded
1980 – 1,057 – Discontinuation of XJ-S considered; John Egan joins Jaguar
1981 – 1,292 – Group 44 second in SCCA TransAm Championship
1982 – 3,111 – HE sales take effect; TWR-Motul XJ-S wins four European Touring Car Championship races
1983 – 4,808
1984 – 6,028 – 3.6 sales take effect; Jaguar privatized; TWR-Jaguar XJ-S wins European Touring Car Championship; four-wheel-drive XJ-S (XJ79) project commences (later abandoned)
1985 – 7,510 – Last full year of Series 3 XJ6; company founder Sir William Lyons dies February, aged 84; TWR-Jaguar XJ-S wins James Hardie 1000, Australia
1986 – 8,838 – XJ40 saloon launched; record year in USA (24,464 cars)

1987 – 9,537 – TWR-Jaguar XJR-8 wins World Championship for Sports Cars
1988 – 10,284 – V12 Convertible a hit in USA; TWR-Jaguar XJR-9LM wins Le Mans; record 51,939 cars produced
1989 – 10,665 – XJ-S record year; Ford takeover of Jaguar
1990 – 9,255 – TWR-Jaguar XJR-12 wins Le Mans
1991 – 4,649 – Venture Pressings come into operation
1992 – 3,638 – Depressed luxury car market UK/US – 20,598 cars produced, lowest annual total since 1981
1993 – 5,192 – XJS floorpan adapted for Aston Martin DB7
1994 – 6,643 – 4.0 Convertible revives US sales
1995 – 5,802 – Last full year of production

Total XJ-S production 1975–1995: 112,052

Notes: Total manual-gearbox XJ-S 5.3 Coupe production 352 (4 in 1975, 130 in 1976, 143 in 1977, 63 in 1978, 12 in 1979). Total Cabriolet production 1,150 (3.6), 3,862 (5.3). Suggested approximate total XJR-S production 300 (5.3), 500 (6.0) including 50 6.0 Convertibles supplied to US in 1992/93.

XJ-S US sales history 1982–1995

Model	82	83	84	85	86	87	88	89	90	91	92	93	94	95
V12 Coupe	1,409	2,705	3,480	3,784	4,310	3,527	2,488	1,901	1,658	1,008	702	139	109	51
V12 Conv						838*	2,014	2,556	3,057	1,730	1,356	348	632	362
4.0 Coupe												613	388	364
4.0 Conv												1,866	3,163	3,758
Total XJS	1,409	2,705	3,480	3,784	4,310	4,365	4,502	4,457	4,715	2,738	2,058	2,966	4,292	4,535

* Hess & Eisenhardt conversions

Performance figures

Type/year tested	GT Coupe 1976[§]	HE Coupe 1982[*][§]	3.6 Coupe 1984/87[†]	V12 6.0 Coupe[‡]	XJR-S 6.0[‡]	XJS 4.0 Coupe[‡]
Mean max speed (mph)	142/153/137	153/140 Fed	134/141	144	155	136
Acceleration (mph/sec)						
0–30	3.2/ 2.8/ 3.8	3.4/ 3.4 Fed	3.1/ 2.6	3.3	2.5	3.4
0–40	4.5/ 3.8/ 6.2	4.6	4.4/ 4.1	4.8	3.7	4.8
0–50	5.9/ 5.1/ 6.7	6.1/ 6.3 Fed	5.8/ 5.6	6.3	4.9	6.6
0–60	7.5/ 6.7/ 8.6	7.5/ 8.2 Fed	7.8/ 7.4	8.0	6.3	8.7
0–70	9.5/ 8.4/11.0	9.2/11.6 Fed	10.0/ 9.9	10.4	8.1	11.1
0–80	11.9/10.5/13.9	11.3/13.5 Fed	12.6/12.4	12.9	10.1	14.1
0–90	14.7/13.4/ –	14.0	16.3/15.3	16.0	12.4	18.0
0–100	18.4/16.2/22.2	16.8/21.3 Fed	20.4/19.7	20.4	15.1	22.8
0–110	23.1/20.2/ –	20.6	26.1/24.6	26.0	18.8	29.4
0–120	30.4/25.8/ –	26.6	37.2/31.8	32.7	23.0	40.3
Standing ¼-mile	15.7/15.0/16.5	15.6/16.3 Fed	16.0/15.9	16.3	14.7	16.7
4th/5th gear (manual)						
10–30	7.5		12.7/ 8.2			
20–40	6.8		11.7/ 7.3			
30–50	6.6		10.6/ 6.7			
40–60			10.6/ 6.9			
50–70	6.8		11.6/ 7.2			
60–80	6.9		12.5/ 7.3			
70–90	7.1		13.9/ 7.1			
80–100	7.2		15.5/ 7.3			
90–110	8.0		16.5/ 8.8			
100–120	10.3		19.0/11.6			
Final-drive ratio	3.07/3.07/3.31	2.88/2.88 Fed	3.54/3.54	2.88	2.88	3.54
Overall mpg (imp)	14/14/13	16.3/14.9 Fed	18.0/18.0	14.5	14.6	18.5
Kerb weight (lb)	3,808	3,808	3,542/3,584	4,055	3,990	3,555

* *Autocar* published an HE Coupe road test (RDU 928W) in April 1982 which gave 0–60mph in 6.5sec and 0–100mph in 15.7sec, while the same magazine found that their 1989 XJR-S returned 9.3sec for 0–60mph, but the figures in the table are thought to be more representative of the HE Coupe over its lifetime.
§ *(Figure sequence: UK automatic/UK manual/Federal automatic)*
† *(Figure sequence: UK automatic/UK manual except where indicated)*
‡ *(Figure sequence: UK automatic)*

APPENDIX G

Specialists and Clubs

Parts and services

Note: Jaguar franchised dealers can supply most parts for cars up to five years old and will be keen to service them (in some cases they can also help with much older vehicles). The level of knowledge on older XJ-Ss at dealerships is variable, though some take a special interest in them. Your nearest franchised dealer will be listed in your telephone directory.

The companies listed here are mainly independent of Jaguar; few specialize exclusively in XJ-Ss (though this may change with time!), but all supply varying degrees of parts and services for the car. The inclusion of a name does not necessarily imply a personal recommendation by the author or publisher, nor any omission to the contrary.

AJ6 ENGINEERING
60 Henshall Road,
Bollington, Macclesfield SK10 5DN
Tel: 01625 573556

V12 and AJ6 engines: management systems, test equipment, tuning parts

ARDEN AUTOMOBILBAU GmbH
Untergath 175,
47805, Krefeld, Germany
Tel: 0049 2151 37230/Fax: 372323

TUV and Jaguar-approved body, chassis and engine conversions; hardtops, parts, accessories, servicing

AUTOSTYLE LTD
Unit 14, Castleview Bus Estate,
Gashouse Road,
Rochester ME1 1PB
Tel: 01634 840530/Fax: 844424

Body conversions (2+2 convertibles, 'wide body', etc), hardtops, round instruments, interior woodwork, etc

ROB BEERE ENGINEERING
Unit 9, Herald Business Park,
Binley, Coventry CV3 2SY
Tel: 01203 650546/Fax: 650539

V12 performance conversions and parts, incl. big-capacity and race

BLACK COUNTRY JAGUARS
Tipton Road,
Dudley,
West Midlands
Tel: 01384 456551/Fax: 456716

Used mechanical, body and trim parts

CLASSIC SPARES
Unit 4, Brook Road,
Britannid Road,
Waltham Cross EN8 7NP
Tel: 01992 716236/Fax: 788424

All parts incl. suspension/steering upgrades, anti-shake kit, etc, plus expert advice

CLIVE SUTTON JAGUAR
14 Kingsbury Trading Estate,
Church Lane,
London NW9 8AU
Tel: 0181 200 4455/Fax: 4094

Sales, service, parts

COACHCRAFT
Stocks Road,
Wittersham TN30 7EJ
Tel: 01797 270210

Coupe to convertible conversions, coachwork, etc

CUSTOM CABRIOS
Chapel Road,
Aldborough, Norwich

Tel: 01263 768824/Fax: 761681

Coupe to convertible conversions, coachwork, repairs

DAVID MANNERS JAGUAR SPARES
991 Wolverhampton Road,
Oldbury, West Midlands B69 4RJ
Tel: 0121 544 4040/Fax: 5558

Parts, mechanical and body

DOUBLE S EXHAUSTS
Station Road,
Cullompton EX16 6NU
Tel: 01884 33454/Fax: 32829

Stainless steel exhausts

DOVE HOUSE JAGUAR
Ware, Herts.
Tel: 01920 438568/Fax: 438452

Specialist used XJ-S retailer

F B COMPONENTS
35 Edgeway Road,
Marston, Oxford OX3 OUA
Tel: 01865 724646/Fax: 250065

Parts

HARVEY-BAILEY ENGINEERING
Ladycroft Farm,
Kniveton, Derby DE6 1JH
Tel: 01335 346419/346440

Handling kit, anti-shake kit for convertible

ROBERT HUGHES
28, Queens Road,
Weybridge KT13 9UT
Tel: 01932 858381/Fax: 857648

Specialist used XJ-S retailer

HYPER PERFORMANCE AND STYLING
Unit 7, Stationfields Estate,
Kidlington OX5 1JD
Tel: 01865 842557/Fax: 842558

Body, chassis and transmission conversions, servicing

LISTER CARS LTD
10 Mole Business Park,
Leatherhead KT22 7AG
Tel: 01372 3774

LYNX MOTORS INT. LTD
68 Castleham Road,
St Leonards on Sea TN38 9NU
Tel: 01424 851277/Fax: 853771

Lynx Eventer estate conversion

PAUL BAILEY DESIGN
Southway Drive,
North Common,
Warmley,
Bristol BS15 5NN
Tel: 0117 935 3222/Fax: 0117 947 7716

Body conversions and coachwork, repairs

TWR/JaguarSport
Decreasing range of JaguarSport parts available from Jaguar franchised dealers

XJS BREAKERS,
Essex
Tel: 01992 768007

Used parts, body and mechanical

CLUBS

Jaguar Drivers' Club Ltd,
18 Stuart Street
Luton LU1 2SL
Tel: 01582 419332

Oldest-established UK club; active XJ Register

Jaguar Enthusiasts' Club,
Membership Secretary,
'Sherborne',
8 Mead Road,
Stoke Gifford,
Bristol BS12 6TS
Tel: 01179 698186

Probably the largest Jaguar club worldwide; emphasis on maintenance/restoration

Jaguar Car Club,

Membership Secretary,
'Barbary', Chobham Road,
Horsell,
Woking GU21 4AS
Tel: 01483 763811

Active competition section, plus social/touring events

USA

There are over 50 local Jaguar clubs in the US; for details of the nearest and of the national JCNA magazine *Jaguar Journal*, please contact:

Jaguar Clubs of North America,
Jerry Parkhill,
9685 McLeod Road
RRNo. 2 Chillinack BC,
Canada V29 6H4

Australia

There are eight Australian clubs, details of which can be obtained from *Australian Jaguar* magazine (see below)

Publications

In addition to club journals, the following independent specialist magazines feature the XJ-S regularly:

Jaguar World,
Kelsey Publishing Ltd,
77 High Street,
Beckenham BR3 1AN
Tel: 0181 650 8351/Fax: 650 8035

Internationally distributed magazine published six times a year. Managing editor Paul Skilleter

Australian Jaguar,
L. H. Hughes,
PO Box 228,
Holland Park
Queensland 4121,
Australia

Published six times a year, also serves as the official journal of the Australian Council of Jaguar Clubs